The book is i
instruction in
climbing, snov
The second part gives a concise but clear
account of the theory behind the essentials, with
a final chapter on the important requirements of
the new Mountain Leadership Certificate. The
text has been 'vetted' by a climbing instructor at
one of Britain's largest mountain centres, and the
technical sketches were drawn by an artist who is
also an expert modern climber.

*Showell Styles*

# The Arrow Book of Climbing

**ARROW BOOKS**

ARROW BOOKS LTD
*178–202 Great Portland Street, London W1*

AN IMPRINT OF THE HUTCHINSON GROUP

London Melbourne Sydney
Auckland Bombay Toronto
Johannesburg New York

*

First published 1966
Arrow edition 1967



*Made and printed in Great Britain
by The Anchor Press Ltd.,
Tiptree, Essex*

# CONTENTS

# 6 CONTENTS

# ILLUSTRATIONS
## BETWEEN PAGES 96 AND 97

# ACKNOWLEDGEMENTS

Among the many who have helped with the matter and illustrations of this book the author owes especial thanks to Mr. Stephen Glass, Instructor at the Snowdonia National Recreation Centre, for his constructive criticism of the mountaineering techniques described; and to Miss Hester Norris, Messrs. P. L. Barratt, Alan Kragh and Peter Mould, and the Norway Tourist Office, for lending photographs without fee.

The author would also like to thank Mr. R. B. Evans for the line drawings.

# INTRODUCTION

This book is in two parts. Part One presents in concise form the basic techniques for dealing with mountains, as now standardised by the schools of climbing instruction. Part Two contains the basic theory behind the techniques, detailed information about the climber's materials and tools, and some account of the varying surfaces and conditions encountered by the mountaineer—a term here used to describe all those who aspire to gain a summit by any route from the easiest to the hardest.

The six chapters in each part are related; for instance, Chapter Two (*Rock-climbing*) in Part One gives the essential instructions for correct use of the climbing rope, while in Chapter Eight (*The Climbing Rope*) of Part Two the functions and nature of the rope are dealt with in greater detail.

Two cautions are necessary. First, printed instructions can only be a preparation for, or complement to, actual experience of climbing in developing skill and safety on mountains. Second, no beginner in climbing should ever attempt to learn the craft alone or with an inexperienced companion. Whether on rock or snow, the skilled leader is the only safeguard against accident until the novice has practised and mastered the basic techniques.

# PART ONE

# Practical Method

# 1

# Mountain-walking

*Approach*

The ascent or crossing of any high and trackless
terrain requires the knowledge and use of mountaincraft in some degree. The cross-country walk
by lane and field-path involves no hazard and
needs no special equipment, but the climb over
moor or open mountainside enters the fringe of
the mountaineer's domain and demands a different
approach, for two reasons: the absence of route
indications and the height above sea-level. Height
gained means that temperature is lower and the
effects of bad weather more serious. A refreshing
breeze in the valley can be a biting wind at 2,000
feet, and the shower that is a harmless incident in
the low-level-walker's day may be mist and driving
rain higher up, drenching and exhausting the
hill-walker and involving him in potential danger, especially if he has no knowledge of map-and-
compass work. Moreover, any emergency is ten
times more serious on rough high ground than it
would be in the valley. A badly blistered heel or

a strained ligament, no great matters in land of lanes and fields, can easily lead to a genuine emergency on moorland or mountain; the walker or his party is slowed up, perhaps overtaken by darkness, possibly forced to spend a night out in the open in adverse weather conditions. There have been many fatalities caused by this sort of accident when the people concerned have been ill-equipped and uninformed.

The approach to any kind of mountain-walking, then, should be one of respect for the different conditions to be expected. Mountains are a 'playground' only for those who know the rules of the game. These rules, formulated over a century of growing experience, must always be observed. On mountains you can find more freedom from care than anywhere else in the world—but you can only be carefree if taking care has become second nature. Taking care means acquiring the 'know-how' *before* you first venture on mountains, and practising it on every subsequent venture.

The first essential is proper equipment.

### Equipment for Mountain-walking

BOOTS must be either well nailed or soled with moulded rubber—Commando or Vibram type. Shoes, nailed or otherwise, are entirely unsuitable. SOCKS AND STOCKINGS should be woollen. Wearing two pairs makes all the difference between foot-weariness and freshness at the end of a long day. The pairs should be the same thickness or one pair will ruck-up under the other. Use an un-darned pair next to the skin.

TROUSERS. Leg-coverings of any sort must first of all be *windproof*. Climbing-breeches are all right, but if jeans are worn a pair of light windproof trousers (e.g. bri-nylon) should be carried in the rucksack. On a warm day in summer shorts are fine—*if* the windproof trousers are also taken along. Girl walkers have already realised that skirts are a nuisance on mountains.

ANORAK. This is an absolute necessity. It should be windproof, long enough to cover the buttocks, and provided with an attached hood. A plastic (not rubberised) anorak, though uncomfortable in nor-mal weather, is excellent in storm or heavy rain.

UNDERCLOTHING. To some extent a matter of personal taste, undergarments are best when of a loose weave or cellular type. Nylon next the skin is bad because it will not absorb body moisture.

SPARE CLOTHING. Whatever is worn on the march, a spare woollen sweater, preferably of the long-sleeved sort, should be carried in the rucksack. For *winter hill-walking* wool gloves, wool scarf, and wool cap or 'balaclava' must be taken as essential spares.

RUCKSACK. A modern light frame rucksack is best for mountain-walking; a frameless sack should be preferred if the day is to include any rock-climbing. Avoid the type of haversack that is slung over one shoulder. In the rucksack there should always be *six essential items*:

> Map
> Compass
> Emergency food
> Basic first-aid outfit
> Whistle
> Spare sweater (already mentioned)

MAP. This will be the one-inch Ordnance Survey map of the area you are walking in. Make sure the map covers *all* the country of your proposed travels, with a margin in case you make some mistake and 'walk off the map'.

COMPASS. Get a good compass to start with and practise using it. A compass on a perspex protractor, such as the Silva Type 2, is the best for normal mountain-walking.

EMERGENCY FOOD. This is carried for emergency use only—exhaustion, benightment on the mountain—and can be glucose tablets, dextrosol, or concentrated sugar food such as Kendal Mint Cake.

BASIC FIRST-AID OUTFIT. It is obviously not possible to carry equipment for dealing with major fractures, etc. The outfit should include small adhesive bandages to cover cuts or raw places (contact of sock on a raw heel can cause blood-poisoning, for instance), a two-inch roller bandage, lint, and such small personal necessities as anti-sunburn cream.

WHISTLE. In serious difficulty on the hills, shouts for help are often misunderstood. The sounding of the Mountain Distress Signal by whistle-blast cannot be misunderstood. It is

Six long blasts in quick succession, then a minute's silence; repeat until help comes.

Some people, the writer among them, make a practice of carrying fifty feet of nylon line or Grade Two rope when walking on mountains. In an emergency it could be immensely useful.

*Using Map and Compass*

The present-day Ordnance Survey map is very easy to read. Briefly, one inch on the map represents one mile on the terrain; the grid lines ruled on the map may be taken as running north-south, east-west; the contour lines show a steep slope when close together, an easy slope when farther apart, and represent a difference of fifty feet in height between each contour. Map North, or True North, is not the same as Magnetic North—to which your compass needle points. To have the

'N' on your compass dial corresponding with True North you must get the needle pointing eight degrees west (to the left) of the 'N'. (This is dealt with in greater detail in Chapter Seven of Part Two, *Route-finding*.)

To 'set' the map, therefore, place the open map flat and the compass on it with the north-south line on the compass parallel to one of the north-south grid lines. Turn map and compass together until the needle points eight degrees west of North. The details on the map now correspond with the details of the landscape round you. On a clear day this may be good enough to give you your onward route. In mist you will need to steer a course.

THE COMPASS IN MIST. The mountain-walker should be able to pin-point his position on the map at any time. This is essential for using the compass in mist. At the first threat of mist, therefore, establish your exact position. Lay the map flat, place the compass on it with its centre exactly over your position, and set the map as described in the last paragraph. Find on the map the objective you want to steer for, and take a straight line from the centre of the compass to that objective. Where the line cuts the edge of the compass dial you will find the direction you have to steer—either as a number or as a compass point, like N.N.W. or S.E. With the Silva protractor-mounted compass you would hold the compass steady and turn the movable protractor until the arrow mark DIRECTION OF TRAVEL points to your objective, and then read off the direction.

An example will make this clearer, with Figure 1 to illustrate it.

We will assume you are on your way up to a summit, A, when mist begins to gather. You halt at X, set the map and find your position, and discover the direction or *bearing* of A from X as already described. The line of bearing cuts the edge of the dial at 145, or a little S. of S.E. By keeping the needle pointing to True North and walking on that bearing, you can reach the summit cairn even in the thickest mist.

ESTIMATING TIME AND DISTANCE. The best method of getting a near estimate is known as Naismith's Rule:

> *Allow twenty minutes for every map-mile and add thirty minutes for every 1,000 feet of height to be climbed.*

Applying this to our example, Figure 1, and assuming you want to reach your summit and then get down out of the mist to the main road, avoiding the crags shown on the map west of Summit A, calculate as follows:[1]

1. Note: in Figure 1 the contour lines are about 200 feet apart.

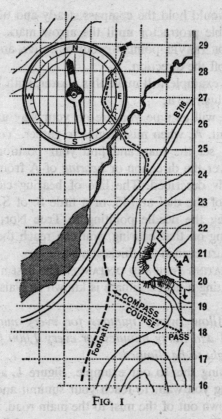

FIG. I

'Summit A bears 145 from my position X, map distance half a mile, 500 feet of ascent—10 minutes plus 15 minutes—I should be at the cairn in 25 minutes.

'I can avoid the crags by descending due south to the pass, 1 map-mile and 800 feet of descent—say 25 minutes at most. Then west-north-west for just over a mile and I'll strike the footpath marked running north to join the main road after another mile—say 40 minutes from the pass.

'My time from X over the summit and down to the main road will be about $1\frac{1}{2}$ hours.'

Note, however, that Naismith's Rule is only accurate when applied to mountain climbs or traverses; it will not work for long near-level tramps over moorland and peat-hags.

Having planned your route and its directions from point to point on the map, and estimated your arrival times at each point so that you can check them, you can safely traverse your mountain in mist.

It is a very good plan to make out a time-distance schedule on these lines before a long mountain walk, and to record it in a notebook with due allowance for halts. An example will be found in Chapter Seven, where also some further guidance in compass work is given.

## Mountain-walking Technique

People accustomed to level roads and pavements use a jerky up-and-down knee action which is as unsuited to mountain terrain as the heel-and-toe

methods of the racing walker. Any unsuitable or
inefficient physical action on mountains is a potential danger because it leads to over-rapid fatigue
or muscular strain; and the mountain-walker, for
his own comfort and enjoyment, should learn and
practise the right way of using his feet on steep
rough ground.

UPHILL. At the very beginning of the day settle into a fairly slow steady pace—a rhythm to be maintained uphill, downhill, and on the level. As the
uphill slope steepens, the rhythm does not change;
the steps become shorter. On a very steep slope
the same rhythm can be kept by taking a slanting
line instead of going straight up. A good mountain-walker plans this slanting line so that it follows the succession of ledges or terraces his accustomed eye has spotted—he does not zigzag just
for the sake of lessening the angle. The ideal is to
place the foot down squarely at every step, the
whole of the sole making the thrust. To spring up
from the toe is entirely wrong; so is trying to traverse along the side of a slope by edging in the
sole—the boot sole should be set down flat against
the slope and the ankle flexed. Looking ahead for
the next or next-but-one spot where the foot can
be placed becomes automatic after a little practice. It saves the stumble and recovery that uses
as much of your energy as fifty sure steps.

DOWNHILL walking employs the same methods, but with a difference in knee action. The smooth down-press and straightening becomes an absorbing of shock on the downhill gradient, and keeping a rigid knee-joint is the shortest and surest way of damaging muscle and ligament. Don't come down jerkily, digging in your heels. Try to place the sole flat, keep the knees slightly bent and springy, move your body down above your feet instead of leaning back. On a fairly steep slope you will find that by leaning slightly forward you can place your boot sole flat on the surface, though you will have to move a little faster. If you are surefooted and your leg-muscles are in perfect trim you can take an exhilarating run down a safe mountainside, but remember that this is a very exacting test for knee and ankle.

Scree-running—on small, loose scree only—is done with the heels digging well in, for the sliding material underfoot absorbs the shock.

### Mountain-walking in Winter

'Winter' may well include part of spring and autumn. Conditions on the mountains can be summer-like, but the swift change of weather will be more serious. The penalty of imprudence or carelessness is always more severe. The RULES must be strictly adhered to.

1. See that the chosen route allows a large margin of time for involuntary halts, so that you will not fail to be off the mountain before dark.

2. Plan the route in advance and note the places on it whence you can descend safely to the valley.

3. If there is *any* snow visible on the hills take an ice-axe and know how to use it (see Chapter Four).

4. Don't start unless you—and everyone with you—are perfectly fit.

5. Take plenty of food, including sweets and chocolate, and add a thermos flask of some hot sweet drink.

6. Be certain your protective clothing is quite adequate for the worst sort of winter weather. Chapter Nine discusses this question in detail.

*Safety Precautions*

These, too, should be regarded as Rules to be invariably followed.

DON'T WALK ALONE in mountains until you have gained a wide experience of mountain-walking in several areas and under varied conditions. An accident is far more serious to the solitary climber than to the member of a small party, or the man with a companion.

ALWAYS leave, with some responsible person, a note of where you propose to go and your expected time of return. If you and your friends start walking from your parked car leave a similar note inside the car, on the seat—*not* tucked under the windscreen-wiper to be blown away.

NEVER trust to your 'sense of direction'; there is no such thing. Use compass and map frequently to check your position.

The last two sections are addressed primarily to the pair of walkers or the small party. Special considerations apply to large parties on mountains, especially to parties of inexperienced youngsters or schoolchildren. The last chapter in this book, *Mountain Leadership,* should be consulted by Leaders of such parties.

# 2

# Rock-climbing

*Approach*

You can enjoy mountains without becoming a rock-climber, but the best of the mountain world will be closed to you unless you acquire a sound knowledge of rock-climbing and snow-climbing technique. It is not necessary to become a 'tiger' on rock-climbing routes of V.S. (Very Severe) standard, unless you have a special aptitude or ambition in that line; capacity to lead a Very Difficult rock climb safely, with an equal efficiency on snow, will bring the best majority of Alpine peaks within your grasp and open the way to other and higher mountains. A genuine dislike of having space below your feet is a good enough reason for leaving rock-climbing alone. We climb solely for our pleasure and it is quite pointless for anyone to force themselves to make an unpleasant or frightening ascent. On the other hand, many people who feel more or less insecure or dizzy with a steep drop beneath them, yet wish to become mountaineers, may take comfort from the fact that this feeling, in nine cases out of ten, does not persist; it passes as the eye accustoms itself to the novel angle and the muscles to the new tensions.

The traditional approach to rock-climbing is as a means of making closer acquaintance with mountains. To many this still seems the natural approach. Today a fair proportion of modern climbers regard rock-climbing as a sport in its own right, having only a secondary relation to the ascent of a mountain. There is nothing to be said against this point of view, but it is as well for the beginner to remember that not all first-rate rock-climbers are first-rate mountaineers.

It is not unusual nowadays for men and girls to begin rock-climbing without any previous experience of mountains. There are many advantages in graduating to the rope from mountain-walking, and one of them is that you will already possess some of the necessary equipment. This has been mentioned in Chapter One. Note that for rock-climbing the rucksack should be a frameless one, and that boots are usually 'Vibs'—soled with moulded rubber. (Some people still prefer a clinker nailing, especially in wet weather; see Chapter Nine for a discussion of this question.) The additional equipment required is given below.

## Equipment for Rock-climbing

The CLIMBING ROPE to use is 120 feet of Grade 4 nylon rope. Normally your leader or instructor on initial climbs will provide the rope.

A hemp WAIST LENGTH will be needed. This is twenty feet (average) of ⅝ in. Italian hemp line.

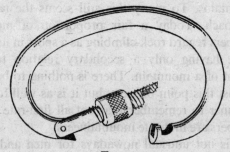

FIG. 2

The SNAP-LINK (commonly known as *krab*, short for *karabiner*) for attachment to the waist length must be of the screw-gate sort shown in Fig 2. It is made so that a rope loop can be clipped into it and the spring clip secured against accidental opening by the screw.

One SLING may be considered sufficient for the medium-grade rock climbs, up to Very Difficult standard. It is a loop of spliced nylon rope (Grade 4, the same size as the climbing rope) about six feet in circumference. To this a second snap-link is attached, of the type shown in Figure

3. If the sling is to be used as an anchor belay, however, it should have a screw-gate. More slings and krabs, of varied sorts, are carried on the higher grade routes.

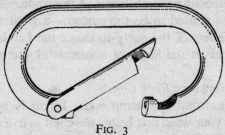

FIG. 3

With rope, waist length, and sling added to *all* the items of equipment listed in Chapter One you are ready to tackle your first rock climb.

*The Leader*

A safe, experienced Leader must be found. Never attempt to do a first climb with an inexperienced companion. Probably the best way of learning rock climbing is by taking a course at a recognised school of mountain instruction, such as one of the Centres of the Central Council for Physical Recreation. Here your Leader will be not only a good climber but also a good instructor, which is essential because your aim is to become a sound Leader yourself.

The Leader of a 'rope' of climbers should be the best climber. In effect he is in command of the party. He climbs first on the rope, has least protection from it, and plays the most important part in overcoming the obstacles of the route. On this account it used to be the custom—a good one—for the rest of the party to thank the Leader for his 'lead' at the finish of a successful climb.

## Procedure on a Rock Climb

PREPARATION. The hemp waist length is wound round your waist just below the chest in five or six turns. The ends are tied with a fisherman's knot (see Figure 4) and can be tucked through the 'lay' of the hemp—between the strands—as a precaution against working loose. A reef knot (Figure 4) can be used instead, and is less bulky. The screw-gate 'krab' is clipped round all the strands of the waist length with the screw-gate downwards. The rope is uncoiled at the foot of the climb, and each end (assuming there are two climbers, the Leader and yourself) is secured to the krab on the waist length of a climber; the knot used is the Tarbuck knot, shown in Figure 4. This knot allows the loop of the rope to be clipped into the krab, and will tighten and slide grudgingly under tension, thus giving an extra margin of safety in the event of a bad fall on the rope.

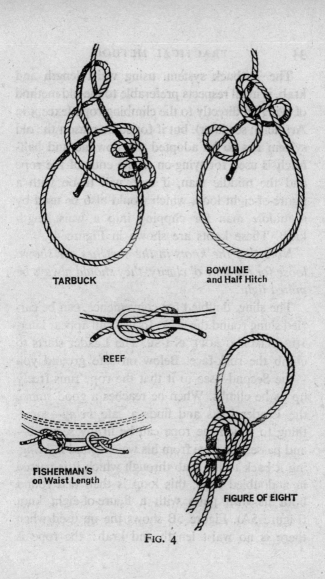

**TARBUCK**

**BOWLINE**
**and Half Hitch**

**REEF**

**FISHERMAN'S**
**on Waist Length**

**FIGURE OF EIGHT**

Fig. 4

The Tarbuck system, using waist length and krab, is in all respects preferable to the old method of tying-on directly to the climbing rope (except in Artificial; see later), but if for some reason the old system has to be adopted the bowline and half-hitch is used for tying-on to the ends of the rope and the middle man, if any, will tie-on with a figure-of-eight loop, which would also be used by a middle man for clipping into a waist-length krab. These knots are shown in Figure 4.

*Note that the knots in the sketches are shown loose for the sake of clarity; they should always be pulled tight.*

The sling, doubled for convenience, can be carried slung round the neck. Its use will appear later.

THE CLIMBING ROPE IN USE. The Leader starts to climb the rock-face. Below on safe ground you —the Second—see to it that the rope runs freely up as he climbs. When he reaches a good *stance* the Leader halts and finds a safe *belay*—something to which the rope can be firmly secured— and passes the rope from his waist round it, bringing it back to his krab through which it is passed in a doubled loop; this loop is then tied round both its own parts with a figure-of-eight knot (Figure 5A). Figure 5B shows the tie used when there is no waist length and krab: the rope is

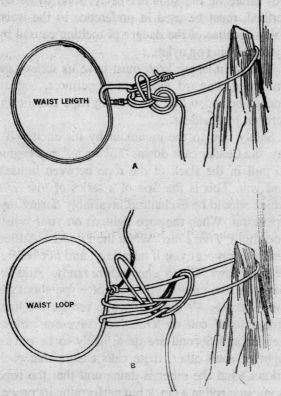

WAIST LENGTH

A

WAIST LOOP

B

FIG. 5

brought back from the belay, passed as a doubled
loop through the waist loop, and then tied round
both its own parts with the figure-of-eight. With

this latter tie the shoulder belay, soon to be described, must be used in preference to the waist belay because of the danger of melting caused by nylon rubbing on nylon.

The waist-length krab must have its screw-gate on the downward side, not uppermost, for an anchor belay, so that the moving rope cannot unscrew it by accident.

Safely tied to the mountain by his anchor belay, the Leader calls down, '*Taking in!*' and begins to pull in the slack of the rope between himself and you. This is the first of a series of *five calls* which should be exchanged invariably during this operation. When the rope tightens on your waist, you shout '*That's me!*' When the Leader is settled ready to support you if necessary, and not before, he calls down '*Climb when you're ready!*' And before you step up on to the rock-face you shout the final warning—'*Climbing!*'—and receive the final 'green light' call of '*O.K.!*' or '*Aye-aye!*' Since Leader and Second are quite likely to be out of sight of each other, these calls ensure that each knows what the other is doing and that the rope is not snagged in a crack but performing its proper duty of safeguarding the man below.

BELAYING. As you climb up, the Leader takes in the rope round his body from hand to hand. If you slip off and dangle on the rope the shock is taken up by the interposed spring and friction of his body and hands, and he himself cannot be pulled off his stance because he is tied to his anchor belay. This principle, of interposing the belayer's body between the moving climber and the anchor belay, is invariable in all belaying with the rope.

The *Leader's Belay* can be a shoulder belay if the Second is coming up from directly below him. If, however, he has made a *traverse*—climbed across the face—so that the Second is off to one side, he will use the waist belay described in the next paragraph and illustrated in Figure 7. For the shoulder belay he takes in the rope under one armpit, up across his back, and down to his other hand (Figure 6). He does not pull, unless the Second asks for a tight rope, but keeps it just taut enough to allow no slack. When the Second reaches the stance and is up beside the Leader his first action is to anchor himself as the Leader did. If you use the same anchor make certain he can afterwards take off his own belay without removing yours; if his loop is placed over a spike or projection, for instance, push your loop up *under* his and then tie it back to your waist. If this is not done there is a moment during the change-over when both of you are belayed.

FIG. 6

The Leader now begins to climb the second *pitch* and your job is to safeguard him.

The *Second's Belay* must be designed to withstand a far greater shock, in the event of a slip and fall, than the Leader's. A Leader falling from twenty feet above the stance will fall forty feet before the belay checks his fall; there is seldom time for the Second to shorten the length of rope run out. A competent Leader on a medium-grade climb is very unlikely to fall, but the whole point of belaying—of all safeguarding on a mountain, in fact—is to guard against the thousandth chance. Give him all your attention, therefore, and plan what you will do if a fall occurs.

Stand firmly facing outwards, with no slack in the loop attaching you to the anchor. The rope from the man above runs through the grasp of one hand, then round the waist above the krab on your waist length and via a single turn round the forearm to the other hand (Figure 7). Pay out the rope freely and carefully as the Leader climbs so that he is never held back or jerked. To arrest a fall bring the hands together in front of the body to increase the friction of the rope round it, slightly bend the knees and brace yourself, grasp the rope only moderately tightly for the first shock and then tighten the grasp to check it completely. By allowing the rope to slide a little at first you lessen the strain on it and the consequent danger of breaking. This, together with the resilience of your body and the Tarbuck knots on your anchor belay and at the Leader's waist, adds enormously to the chances of arresting a fall successfully.

Many Seconds wear leather gloves to save their hands in the event of a Leader's fall, and in ad-

FIG. 7

vanced rock-climbing, where the possibility of a
Leader's falling is increased, gloves should be
standard equipment. Leather gauntlets are best.

Pitch by pitch (a pitch being the stretch of rock
between two stances) the climb continues, each
climber safeguarding the other by belaying, until you reach the final pitch and the easy ground
above where the rope can be taken off. On the
climb some other ways of safeguarding with the
rope may have been used.

OTHER BELAYS. The sound spike, bollard, or projection is the most common form of anchor on a rock stance. The climber always makes certain, before belaying to it, that it will withstand the greatest strain, and sees to it that his point of attachment is high up—above waist-level at least. If the only good anchor is low down he may have to sit or crouch to use it safely. Instead of a rock spike there may be a crack near the stance with a stone jammed firmly in it. This can be used for a *Thread Belay*. The loop of climbing rope is threaded round the stone, brought back to the waist-length krab, and secured there with a figure-of-eight knot. Or—a method which is usually simpler and handier—the sling is brought into use as shown in Figure 8. Never pass the sling 'through itself' but always clip both loops of it into its krab. Then clip in the climbing rope from your waist and tie back as in Figure 5.

A *Running Belay* is sometimes used by the Leader for additional safeguarding on a long pitch or an awkward step. This is the main use of the sling. If a convenient projection offers, the sling is hung over it with the krab attached, and the climbing rope is then clipped into the krab to run through it as the climber moves on (Figure 9). If he now slips, the climber will only fall twice the distance between himself and his running

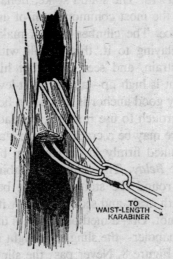

TO
WAIST-LENGTH
KARABINER

Fig. 8

belay. There are rules to be observed when a running belay is used:

1. The climbing rope must run through the krab, never through the sling itself.

2. The Leader must warn his Second when he proposes to put on a 'runner', so that the Second can prepare himself for the *upward* pull which would be the result of a fall.

3. Whenever possible, the anchor belay must be contrived to withstand a pull upward as well as downward; a thread belay will do this.

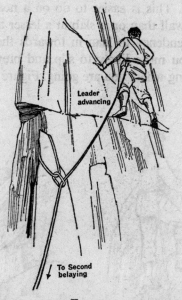

Leader
advancing

To Second
belaying

FIG. 9

It is never advisable, however, for the Second
to change his anchor belay during the Leader's
ascent unless the Leader can anchor himself securely while the change is being made.

*The Basic Technique of Rock-climbing*
On all mountain surfaces, and in all forms of
climbing except Artificial, your aim should be always to stand and move in balance above your

footholds. This is easier to do on a nearly vertical rock-wall than on a slab at a lesser angle. Resist the tendency to lean in towards the rock; it makes you more likely to slip and prevents you from seeing where you are going. Figure 10 shows

FIG. 10

the right posture (a) and the unsafe foothold you have when you lean inward off balance (b).

As Second on a first rock climb, or under instruction, it is essential to watch closely how the Leader tackles the pitch, especially where and how he places his feet. The safest and easiest progress is made by using footholds properly, not by swarming up on big 'jug-handle' holds for the hands. Handholds have to be pulled on sometimes, and indeed all parts of the body come into play in dealing with the varied problems of a climbing route; but the human leg-muscles are the best developed of all to support the body's weight.

You will climb safely and well if you remember the following rules:

Plan your moves on as much as you can see of the pitch, before you begin to climb it.

Look for footholds first and see that your boot uses them in the best possible way.

Move up as smoothly and continuously as you can without hurrying or skimping.

Use handholds for keeping yourself in balance only, unless it is really necessary to pull on them.

Avoid long upward steps or reaches; use the small intermediate foothold between two large footholds far apart, and the fingertip handhold at chest-level rather than the jug-handle at arm's length overhead.

Some or all of these rules will have to be modified when the climb ceases to be a straightforward rock-face and provides one of those varied obstacles—no two of which are ever the same —to be encountered on most routes.

The WALL—a near-vertical face—will require more than a balancing touch on handholds. There may be incuts—small holes or pockets in the rock —or ledges for the fingertips, projecting knobs, or vertical ridges where a pinch-grip provides just sufficient support. Settle the fingers on the hold so as to get the most efficient support from it to hold you from falling backwards. Then use foot-hold to make the upward movement.

SLABS occur when a flat rock-wall leans back at an easier angle. Remember to keep the body upright in balance. Beginners find this difficult to do when traversing (moving horizontally) on a slab. The holds will tend to be small rounded bosses or thin awkwardly angled cracks, but they can be used safely when your weight is vertically above them, so keep erect above your toes and use low-level handholds.

CHIMNEYS are deep clefts, usually in a vertical wall, into which you can get your whole body. Chimneying technique is best learned by trial and practice, but the basic principle is the use of friction. In a narrow chimney you jam your back against one wall by pressure of knees against the other; slide your back up a little way, using your hands wherever they are most useful; bring up the knees to jam again; and so on. In a wider chimney you can get your boot soles against one wall and your back and hands against the other, and alternately 'walk up' the boots and hitch up the back (Figure 11). In a chimney too wide for this you may be able to *bridge*, maintaining position

FIG. 11

by the opposing pressures of one foot and one hand on either wall and moving up each point of attachment in turn. Large boulders or *chockstones* are sometimes jammed in the upper part of the chimney and the easiest route may go behind the chockstone. One wall of a chimney often offers better hold than the other, or an easier finish at the top; before starting consider which way to face.

CRACKS are clefts too small to take the climber's body. You may be able to jam one leg and one arm in a crack, using the other limbs to get hold on the outside wall. If it is narrower than this it can probably be climbed by using jamming holds for boots and hands. The boot is inserted in the crack and turned until it grips; if it is jammed in flat you may find it impossible to release it. One way of getting hand hold on a narrow crack is to pull outwards with the fingers of either hand on the opposing sides of the fissure.

The MANTELSHELF is usually a narrow ledge on a vertical wall with another steep wall rising behind it. It can often be climbed by getting both hands flat on the ledge, fingers turned inwards, and pressing up until one leg can be raised to get foothold on the ledge. A knee can be used, but it is a good rule to avoid using a knee on a hold because when it is there you cannot raise yourself any higher.

DESCENT of a rock climb should be done occasionally; ideally, and in preparation for Alpine climbing, climbing down should be done as often as climbing up. Most people find climbing down harder at first, but there are some advantages which you will soon discover. Instead of pushing against gravity you are using gravity and merely checking its action. Instead of climbing in ignorance of the nature of the holds overhead you can often look down on them from the top of the pitch. On a difficult descent you can sometimes abseil (rope down) as described in the next section.

The belaying procedure is as for ascent, in reverse—the Leader descending last. This puts the burden of route-finding on the first man down. On any but very steep rock, descend facing outwards, or half-sideways, otherwise it is difficult to see your next foothold; but remember that a boot heel is far less safe on a hold than the toe or edge of the sole, and don't come down relying on heels and breeches-seat. Pressure handholds, taken with the palms downwards at waist-level, are immensely helpful in descent.

The ABSEIL method should be learned and practised even though you have little expectation of using it. It may be the means of getting you out of trouble if you decide to retreat from a climb that has proved too hard for you, and it is an essential technique on many Alpine routes. In abseiling the rope is used doubled, the loop at the centre being placed round a *safe* projection or clipped into a krab on a sling placed round the projection.

The ends hang straight down the rock-face. *It is most important to be sure that the rock-spike or bollard is absolutely firm and that the rope will not slip off it.* Nothing (except support from an extra rope above) can avert a very bad accident if the abseil rope comes off.

The sling method is the easiest and most comfortable:

Make a figure-of-eight with the sling and clip the krab (one with a screw-gate should be used) round the two parts of the sling where they cross.

Pull the two loops up round the thighs, under the buttocks, and hold the clipped-on krab in front.

Facing the belay point, pick up the double rope and clip it into the krab, placing the two parts that hang down the rock-face over your right shoulder to run down across your back to your left hand.[1]

Stand on the edge of the drop with your back to it and lean outwards against the pull of the ropes, allowing them to slide through your left hand and round your body, until your legs are pushing almost horizontally against the rock.

Walk backwards down the face, using the left hand to control your speed and your right hand, on the ropes in front of you, for balance only. Knees should be slightly bent, feet a foot or more apart.

1. *Left* and *right* in this description can be reversed if preferred.

By bringing your left hand forward and inward and tightening its grip you can increase friction and stop at any time. A *free abseil* straight down from an overhang can be done easily and

FIG. 12

safely by this method, so effective is the friction (Figure 12).

Pads should be contrived wherever the abseil ropes have to pass over a sharp rock-edge. The rope will have to be recovered by hauling on one end from below. If there is any doubt about its running freely, a sling should be used on the belay point and the rope run through a krab on it. This will mean abandoning sling and krab, but that is better than having to abandon the rope.

The 'classic' method of abseil is worth knowing in case you ever have to rope-down without a sling; you may have used your only sling as described above, for instance. The doubled rope is placed safely round the belay point. You stand astride it facing the belay; pick up both ropes from behind you and bring them round outside your left thigh; lead them across your chest and down over your right shoulder to be grasped behind you with your left hand. Your right hand grasps the ropes in front of you lightly and you walk backwards down the rock as described for the sling method (Figure 13). The classic method gives even more friction but is slower and more painful than the sling method.

### The Grading of Rock-climbing Routes

It has been said that the basic technique just described is adequate for rock climbs up to Very Difficult standard. Guidebooks to the climbing routes of Britain are published, and in these the climbs are classified in five grades of difficulty: Moderate, Difficult, Very Difficult, Severe, Very Severe. A sixth grade, Extremely Severe or XS,

FIG. 13

has been added and indicates the top limit of achievement. These grades are sometimes qualified within their standard—Mild, Very Difficult or Hard Severe, for example. They are for *free-climbing,* in which no artificial aids are used, and refer to ascents made in reasonable weather on dry rock. The nature of some routes is such that they become much harder when the rock is wet, especially when the climber is wearing moulded-rubber soles; and a high wind or cold weather will make most routes harder. This should be remembered when planning the day's climbing.

Climbing guidebooks are useful to the beginner because they enable him to judge beforehand which routes are likely to be within his powers at each stage of his climbing progress. The grades should be regarded as an indication of difficulty only. One man's V.Diff is another man's Severe, for some people who are happy on a slab of Very Difficult standard can be beaten by a chimney graded the same in the guidebook. On big rock-faces like Lliwedd, where the different routes are close together and sometimes cross or join, the guidebook helps to prevent you from getting lost or stuck.

*Protective Headgear*

This additional item of rock-climbing equipment is briefly described in Chapter Nine. A mountaineering helmet, resembling the light padded helmet of the motor-cyclist, is being increasingly worn by climbers on the higher grade British routes and on the Continent. It is not yet common or standard equipment for climbers on the medium-grade climbs in Britain, where the rock is normally sound and stone-falls rarely occur. The increasing numbers of climbers in Britain increases the danger of the dislodged stone; and the worst injuries incurred by a falling climber are head injuries. These two facts make it probable that sooner or later the padded helmet will come to be regarded as essential equipment for all prudent climbers.

## Obtaining Equipment

When getting the equipment mentioned in this chapter and Chapters Three and Four, go to a reputable supplier of mountaineering requirements. Climbing boots should be fitted in the store if at all possible, over two pairs of socks. Make sure that your snap-links conform to the specification laid down by the British Mountaineering Council, and don't use ex-W.D. snap-links, which are unreliable. Finally, take care of all your climbing equipment; examine and check it frequently; and *never lend it*.

# 3

# Advanced Rock-climbing and Artificial

It will have been noticed that in the rock-climbing technique so far described the rope is used purely as a safety precaution, never as a direct aid to progress up the climb. In other words, the rock-face could be climbed without using a rope at all. It will also have been observed that the technique of using hands and feet is comparatively simple. A man whose life depended on climbing a Very Difficult route solo would probably succeed even though he was ignorant of the technique, provided that he was physically fit and properly shod; it would be a desperate and dangerous climb and bad mountaineering, but he would get up somehow. Above Very Difficult standard the rock route is likely to provide obstacles that demand a more specific skill based on knowledge and practice. Severe and Very Severe climbs tend also to have longer run-outs of rope between the stances, more *exposure* (space below the climber's feet), and smaller and sparser holds. Somewhere be-

tween the Very Difficult and Severe gradings you
progress, it may be said, to advanced rock-climbing.

We are still speaking of free-climbing—reliance
on your own boots and fingertips. But it is obvious that as harder and steeper rock-faces are attempted there will occur places where the most
skilled free-climber will be brought to a full stop;
overhangs, smooth walls completely devoid of
holds. Such passages can only be overcome if the
climber can be hoisted up them by direct aid or
contrive an artificial hold for hand or foot. This
he can often do by hammering a metal peg (*piton*)
into a handy crevice. If he can get his peg in firmly
at arm's length overhead, and clip a krab to the
ring in its head, he can lift the rope attached to his
waist and clip it into the krab. Then his Second,
by hauling on the rope from below, can hoist
him as on a pulley for several feet until he can
reach the rock holds above or insert a second piton
for the process to be repeated. This is the basic
principle of artificial climbing, sometimes called
peg-climbing but more commonly known simply
as Artificial.

Pitons are occasionally used to provide extra
protection on the advanced free-climbing routes,
but it is an unwritten rule that pitons should not be
used for direct aid on a route that can be climbed

'free'. The climber on these routes should have mastered the additional technique of using apparently useless holds, especially the *jamming hold*.

FIG. 14

JAMMING. Toe-jamming in very thin cracks is an art in itself and can often be learned by practising assiduously on a suitable crack at a safe distance above the ground. The typical jamming hold, however, is a handhold. Hand-jams and finger-jams can be extremely useful and may provide the vital hold for passing an overhang.

The *hand-jam* utilises a smooth and otherwise holdless crack of, say, three inches in width. Insert the hand sideways, knuckles and back against one side and fingers and ball of thumb against the other. Flex all the hand muscles; the friction obtained by the opposing pressures is astonishing and can provide a hold as sound as a jug-handle

(Figure 14A). An alternative method is to double the thumb across the base of the fingers.

The *finger-jam* can be used in a very narrow vertical crack less than an inch wide. Insert the forefinger with the second finger above it pressing it down (Figure 14B).

The *fist-jam*, an obvious way of using a vertical crack four or five inches wide, gives a perfect hold when the crack narrows slightly downwards (Figure 14D).

The *sprag*, used in a very thin corner crack where one wall protrudes, gives a useful balancing hold. Insert the fingertips and get an opposing pressure with the thumb on the outside wall (Figure 14C).

In larger cracks of various sorts and sizes *arm-jams* are used. The same principle, of obtaining support by jamming with opposing pressures, is the key.

A long crack up which jamming is the only means of progress occurs on quite a number of routes, but these are almost certain to be graded Very Severe.

OTHER HOLDS IN ADVANCED CLIMBING. Besides the use of jamming holds, advanced free-climbing requires an extended skill in the use of holds on the rock surface. The ability to move in balance on good small holds is not enough; progress may have to be made on holds none of which is good enough, alone, to support boot or fingers. The difficulty here is overcome by applying tensions and pressures of the limbs to convert two, or three, inadequate holds into good temporary support. The circumstances are of course infinitely variable, but by way of illustration we can tackle an imaginary problem. A step has to be made across a vertical wall where the only foothold is too small and sloping to support a boot and there are no handholds over which you can hook your fingers. In reach above the bad foothold, however, is a small overhanging flake and farther across the wall to the left is a tiny vertical corner in the rock, half an inch deep—two handholds that are both quite inadequate for any downward pull. But your right hand pushed up under the overhanging flake can get an outward pull, and by opposing this to the inward pressure of your boot against the bad foothold you can make your foot stay in place while you hook your left-hand fingertips round the vertical corner and take the next step to the good foothold beyond.

A note on the *Layback* (Figure 15): the sketch adequately shows this opposing-pressure method of climbing a holdless crack, especially a corner crack or a crack where one of the sides projects beyond the other. It is the most exhausting form of progress in free climbing, and whenever possible it is best to climb such cracks by the less fatiguing method of toe and hand jamming.

PROTECTION IN ADVANCED CLIMBING. Added steepness and exposure and more difficult movement make extra protection desirable for the Leader in advanced climbing. For this he usually carries extra rope slings and krabs, often half a dozen or more, and places a 'runner' (see under *Running Belay* in Chapter Two) when the route suggests it and there is a projection handy. With a succession of well-placed runners behind him he gains confidence for finishing a long and difficult pitch and increased protection in the event of his fall.

It is a sound rule that the rope of the sling should be the same strength as the climbing rope. But on some routes there are projections, nicely positioned for a useful runner, round which the Grade 4 nylon cannot be placed safely because it is too thick. A thinner sling, perhaps of Grade 2 nylon, would fit snugly without danger of slipping off. The Leader may carry slings of several thicknesses so as to make use of such places. The chances of a sling breaking under a fall when it is of thinner rope are, of course, increased, but so long as he bears in mind the weak link behind him the Leader is justified in breaking the general rule;

a good runner on a thin sling is better than none at all.

FIG. 15

Stances without a good anchor belay occur on some hard routes, but often there is a crack somewhere in reach where a thread belay could be contrived if only there was a jammed stone to thread the rope round. Developing from the carrying-up of special stones to jam in such cracks, the device of knotting the rope and jamming the knot to make an anchorage followed. A more modern idea is to use hexagonal steel nuts with the thread smoothed out of the centre hole. Brass or alloy nuts can distort or shear and should not be used. Usually nylon Grade 1 or Grade 2 has to be used for the sling passing through the nut, and two or three nuts of different sizes on one sling are handy. The nut will jam nicely in a crack or slot of the right size and the anchor belay can be made to a krab on the sling. Some XS routes have been climbed using jammed-nut slings to supply hand-holds where none exist; but this is really crossing the borderline from free-climbing to Artificial.

## Artificial Climbing

Artificial, much more than pure rock-climbing, has recently tended to develop into a pastime separate from mountaineering and practised solely for its own sake. It has made safe climbing possible on limestone cliffs and sea cliffs like those of the Dorset coast, where the surface holds are un-sound and dangerous. Its place in the wider craft of mountaineering is secure because its technique has opened magnificent Alpine routes previously closed to climbers by passages impossible using ordinary free-climbing methods.

The development in technique and equipment

of this comparatively new craft is still going on, and it will be some time before the final and definitive textbook of Artificial is written. Here the basic method will be described briefly. Special equipment will of course be needed.

EQUIPMENT FOR ARTIFICIAL. The *rope* normally used is 200 feet of Grade 4 nylon, half of it coloured red, or two 100-foot ropes, one red and one white. Some Artificial climbers prefer Grade 3 rope on account of its lighter weight, others swear by rope with a braided sheath which runs more easily through krabs. Two is the usual number of climbers for an Artificial route.

At least three *slings* with krabs attached will be carried by each climber.

*Étriers,* short ladders of plaited Terylene or similar rope, with two, three, or four steel rungs at least an inch broad, are needed, the number of étriers depending on the nature of the route to be climbed.

A *piton hammer* (Figure 16A) is essential for driving in the pegs.

*Pitons* (pegs) are carried in ample supply, according to the length of the route. They are metal pegs with a flat blade, hard metal for soft rock, softer metal for hard rock. There are many types, two of which are illustrated (Figure 16 B, C), but the piton with its ring at right-angles to the blade

FIG. 16

can be considered standard. Hardwood *wedges* (Figure 16D) are taken for use in wider cracks. The fashion in pitons changes progressively, and the rapid development of Artificial in the United States may soon lead to the introduction of such attachment-points as Bongs, Golos, Rurps, and Crack tacks. Rawlplugs and coach-bolts have been used on limestone faces in this country.

*Krabs.* A great many of these may be needed. The krab on the climber's waist length is of the screw-gate sort, but the rest are the type illustrated in Figure 3, Chapter Two. They should be large enough to take two étriers and the rope and still leave room for fingers to grip through the ring. The catch on the spring-gate, which engages with the body of the krab, tends to prevent the gate from opening when weight is suspended from the krab—a disadvantage when other ropes have to be clipped in. If the krab conforms to the accepted specifications of strength the catch can be dispensed with.

*Footwear.* Light moulded rubber-soled boots, or kletterschuhe, are best. Rubbers are too thin and soft for standing in étriers.

*Other Equipment.* Various gadgets, recently described by a noted Artificial climber as 'junk', are to some extent matters of taste and preference. The most useful extra is probably the 'cow's tail', a small sling clipped to the climber's waist length; it can be clipped into the piton krab for support, freeing the hands. 'Fifi-hooks' are used by some for easier recovery of the étriers below (Figure 17). Others contend that the fifi-hook frequently jams or catches and is more nuisance than help, and use krabs instead. On the long Artificial routes in the Dolomites bivouacs are sometimes necessary on the face, and a proofed tent-sack, with extra food and clothing, will then have to be carried.

### Procedure on an Artificial Climb

We assume two climbers at the foot of a rock-face some hundreds of feet high. From the start, and throughout most of its height, the rock-face is vertical or overhanging and is unclimbable by

LINE TO CLIMBERS
WAIST LIFTS ETRIER
FROM PITON
AS HE MOVES UP

------ ETRIER ------

FIG. 17

free-climbing methods. Cracks and niches, not usable for hands and feet, occur on the face.

The Leader carries three étriers with krabs attached, ten or twelve other krabs, and a score or so of pegs arranged so that he can quickly detach them. His piton hammer hangs by its safety sling from his shoulder and is tucked into a pocket— a rule-pocket in the breeches is useful. He has a cow's-tail loop clipped to his waist length by a separate krab. The two 100-foot ropes, red and white, are tied to his waist with bowline and half-hitch; the Tarbuck system of attachment is not used because it prevents close pulling-up to the pitons.

The Second is tied-on similarly to the ropes. He carries three étriers, piton hammer, spare krabs, and wooden wedges, and he also has a cow's tail.

Having planned his route as far as possible, the Leader selects a convenient fissure high up and hammers in his first peg. If each blow produces a clear ringing note ascending in the musical scale as the peg is driven farther in, he knows it is gripping. He tests it, clips a krab to it, and lifts the red rope to clip it into the krab. In the diagram (Figure 18) this peg is numbered 1. The Leader now clips an étrier to the krab on Peg 1. He calls to his Second: 'Tension red!' The Second hauls on the red rope, pulling the Leader (who assists himself with his feet if he can and with the krab as handhold) up close to Peg 1. The Leader stands on the étrier and clips his cow's tail into the krab to support him upright. From this position he can reach his hands to a crack higher up the rock face, and in this he places Peg 2, driving it well home. He attaches a krab, raises the slack white rope and clips it into the krab, and attaches a second étrier. He calls: 'Tension white, slack red!' and

RED

WHITE

FIG. 18

detaches his cows' tail. The Second's haul on the white rope raises him until he can stand on the second étrier and clip his cow's tail to the krab. And the sequence is repeated until the Leader decides to make a stance and bring the Second up.

*Belaying* on an Artificial route depends on the nature of the stance. If there is a ledge for the feet, or other natural stance, the Leader attaches himself securely and belays his Second as in free-climbing. If he has to make a stance on étriers alone the safest belaying procedure is to drive in an extra peg above him, attach a krab, and clip the moving rope into it so that he belays as over a pulley.

The Second has the laborious task of removing the pegs as he climbs up. His étriers make it easier to do this, since he has to move up past the peg before it can be taken out; from an étrier suspended from the next peg he can make the repeated hammer-blows that will probably be needed to loosen the peg below.

*Horizontal overhangs* or 'roofs' can be overcome by pegging out along the underside of the roof with tension on alternate red and white rope as just described. The Leader will hang free on his étriers, moving them out stage by stage until he can drive in a peg above the overhang. Well-driven pitons will support a man's weight safely even when the pull is directly downwards, the soft alloy peg shown in Figure 16C being particularly effective for this use in hard-rock cracks.

Generally speaking, Artificial demands more strength and endurance than free-climbing, and good nerves. It is done at a much slower pace and is more exhausting physically under conditions of wet or cold. Bad accidents in Artificial climbing have so far proved extremely rare, and it may be considered a safer form than free-climbing when the proper skill is applied.

**4**

# British Snow- and Ice-climbing

*Approach*

Snow and ice on British hills are seasonal pheno-
mena and are markedly different from the snow
and ice of greater mountains like the Alps. British
ice-climbing, to some extent a specialist's sport,
is excellent preparation for the ice pitches found
on many high-grade Alpine routes, but oppor-
tunities for long climbs on snow resembling an
Alpine route are few and far between and in some
seasons may not occur at all south of the Scottish
Highlands. It is not possible to acquire complete
competence for greater mountaineering without
leaving Britain; but it *is* possible, and essential to
every user of winter mountains, to learn how to
use an ice-axe.

Snow-climbing routes such as the gullies of Ben
Nevis give real sport of medium standard in a
good season and their cornices can provide a hard
finish. Steep hard snow-slopes can sometimes be
found. The *arête* (narrow high-angled ridge) of

hard-frozen snow, *névé,* which occurs so often on big Alpine routes, has no counterpart in this country, and of course there are no glaciers. The *crampons* (ice-claws), which are an essential of Alpine equipment, are seldom if ever used on British snow, though they are frequently used on the high-grade British ice climbs. In short, snow in Britain is regarded by most climbers either as an opportunity for practising in preparation for a hoped-for Alpine holiday or as the medium that transforms their summer mountain routes into ways of greater beauty and greater hazard.

*Snow and the Ice-axe*

The material and the implement are so closely linked that they may well share the heading. In the chapter on mountain-walking it was said: 'If there is *any* snow visible on the hills, take an ice-axe and know how to use it.' This instruction can be briefly amplified here. There is always more snow high up than you can see from the valley. Sometimes (and this applies particularly in North Wales and the Lakes) the south-facing slopes may display no white at all when the northern slopes are still snow-covered. Moreover, snow and ice stay longest on paths, and when the paths cross steep mountainside there are often places that can be passed safely with an axe but only hazardously without one. The hill-walker in winter, even if he has no intention of leaving the normally easy path, has need of an axe when there is snow about.

The English name 'ice-axe' (German *pickel*, French *piolet*) suggests that the use of the axe is in cutting steps up a steep ice-slope. This is, in practice, about its rarest use. Its importance in Britain is as a means of attachment to the surface of a snow-covered mountainside. On steep or hard snow neither hands nor boots can perform the functions of supporting the climber against the pull of gravity as they do on summer mountains. To cross a snow-slope safely or climb it, to provide anchorage when there is no other belay, are two of the axe's important uses. A third, and most important of all to the mountain-walker, is as a brake for arresting the slide that could be (and frequently has been) fatal to an axeless climber. For anyone who proposes to go on mountains in snow, by whatever route, the ice-axe is thus one additional item of equipment that should never be left behind.

The ICE-AXE is normally of walking-stick length, of straight-grained ash oval in section, with a spiked ferrule at one end and a steel head at the other. The head has a pick about seven inches long and an adze at least two and a half inches broad. The weight should be two and a half to three pounds.

It is a bad investment to buy a cheap one. The sliding-ring and wrist-sling attached to some axes have disadvantages that balance their advantages. Many climbers dispense with the wrist-sling altogether.

The mountain-walker will be carrying his axe until he reaches the snowline, with the point to the front and the axe-head tucked under his arm; the man in line behind him on the path will certainly complain loudly if the point is to the rear. On easy snow, use the axe like a walking-stick. In crossing a slope of snow, hold the axe with the hand nearest the slope. On a steeper slope, where steps may be kicked, hold the axe across the body with the point towards the slope, ready to take a balancing touch or a deeper thrust to check a slip. If the snow hardens and steps have to be made, slash them with the adze, grasping the shaft in the hand away from the slope, and balance with the spike against the slope as you move from step to step.

CHECKING A FALL. It is very often not realised that on a snow-slope of any steepness and hardness a sliding body accelerates very rapidly. The slope may run out gently into scree or boulders at the bottom, but a man sliding helplessly will be going so fast when he hits them that he is certain to be seriously or fatally injured. It is vital to arrest the slide as quickly as possible, and here the axe can be extremely efficient. The method is not easy unless you have practised it beforehand. When you go out on snow with your axe for the first time make a point of seeking out a steep hard slope—a short ice-slope if possible—with a safe landing at the bottom; practise sliding and checking the fall with the axe, as described below, until you perform the actions swiftly and instinctively.

The fall has occurred in the past to solo walkers or members of an unroped party on a frozen slope. The initial slip is often unexpected. You are prepared for it if you are walking with the ice-axe properly held: a right-handed climber grasps the head with the pick to the rear and his thumb and forefinger round the narrows of the adze, so that his four right-hand fingers are over the top of the head.

Your feet fly from under you; you begin to slide, but you have retained hold of your only hope—the axe.

At once throw yourself on your stomach, face to the slope, at the same time grasping the axe-shaft with your left hand about a foot above the spike.

Bring the right hand grasping the axe-head to the level of the shoulder to left or right, whichever is quicker and handier (to the left is better where

Fig. 19

possible) with the axe-head flat to the slope and the shaft point down it.

Immediately—but gradually—turn the right wrist so as to force the pick to bite into the surface, gripping with all your strength as you do it.

As soon as the speed of the slide begins to be arrested, increase the 'bite' of the pick (Figure 19).

Remember (a) that these actions must be performed immediately the fall occurs, otherwise the rapid acceleration will make the axe-brake hard or impossible to operate; and (b) that to jab the pick in straight away is likely to result in the axe being snatched irresistibly from your grip.

On slopes of such steepness and hardness a party of climbers will usually be roped together. Each man will be properly equipped for winter mountaineering.

### Equipment for British Mountains in Winter

Additional to the ice-axe and the normal mountain equipment mentioned in Chapter One, the winter climber will need some extras.

GLOVES. The sensitivity of the hands to cold varies a great deal in human beings. Generally woollen gloves with a wind-proof outer gauntlet provide adequate protection; but a spare pair of woollen gloves should always be carried.

BOOTS. Vibrams, invariably worn in the Alps (where crampons are put on for the steep hard slopes of snow-ice), are not always the safest sole for British winter climbing. On frozen scree or turf, on rocks covered with slush or thin new snow, they are definitely inefficient. A British ridge like the Crib Goch ridge on Snowdon, though it can provide a splendid near-Alpine route in winter and an easy scramble in summer, is often the scene of narrow escapes when Vibram-soled boots are used on the ice-glazed rocks of cold weather or the slushy ledges of a thaw. In such conditions, and for the varied surfaces that may be encountered in one winter day's mountain-walking, clinker-nailed boots are undoubtedly the safest wear.

CLOTHING. Obviously something warmer than summer wear must be used. An extra sweater besides the spare one in the sack; a woollen scarf to close that vulnerable gap at the neck; a woollen cap or helmet. For those whose skins can take it, woollen underwear is incomparable for beating the numbing chill on the ridge or summit after a sweaty climb up the sheltered slopes.

FOOD. Take as much sugary food as you can: sweets, chocolate, mint cake. A thermos of hot sweet coffee is worth its place in the sack. In bad winter weather the key to maintaining warmth and energy—and therefore safety—is to have a pocketful of glucose sweets and suck them continuously; there will be little opportunity for a long halt and a big intake of food.

ROPE. A 120-foot length of Grade 4 nylon rope is normally sufficient for three climbers.

## Note on Cornices

These wind-formed overhangs of snow occur on the rim of a ridge or the lip of a gully. In time of thaw, or with a warm wind blowing, they become unstable and a danger to climbers ascending the slope or gully. Their danger to mountain-walkers is that they are often not visible to anyone going along the ridge, where the most level footing may be along the crest of a line of cornices above the overhangs. In Figure 20 the leading walker has suddenly perceived the dangerous route he has been following and turned away from the verge. His onward route, a safe one, is represented by the dotted line, keeping well down the slope below the point where it would fracture if the cornice collapsed.

## The Climbing Rope on Snow

On moderate slopes of good snow where steps can be kicked the party moves up in single file, unroped. When a slip seems possible, and its results might be serious, the rope is tied on as described in Chapter Two, *Rock-climbing*. The climbers continue to move together at intervals of twenty or thirty feet, each man holding the coils of slack and not allowing the rope to drag on the snow. The steps made by the Leader should be followed exactly. If the surface hardens, and makes kicking laborious, the Leader slashes steps with the axe-adze as he advances, cutting with one hand (the one away from the slope) and using one hard, well-placed stroke; the firm planting of the boot com-

FIG. 20

pletes the step. A fall can be checked by driving the axe-shaft hard in and taking a turn of the rope round it, but this method should be adopted only in continuous-movement ascent of comparatively easy snow. When the slope becomes steeper or harder, step-cutting more arduous, or the position more hazardous, proper belaying is adopted and the climbers move one at a time.

FIG. 21

BELAYING ON SNOW. The method is entirely similar to belaying on a rock climb, the deep-thrust axe providing the anchor. If a belay is considered necessary at all, it is futile to use any but the best belay available; therefore the interposition of the climber's body between anchor and moving man should be made invariable. The direct axe belay— the rope coming directly from the ascending Leader to the axe—has been proved many times to be a bad method. In two recent cases of fatal falls the axe was jerked from its hole in the snow, and in another case the shaft snapped. The driven axe must be regarded as the anchor for the man who is belaying, and in the event of a fall he must absorb the shock with his own hands and body. Remember that the best of axe belays is always less firm than a good rock bollard.

In belaying the Leader's advance drive in the axe at a point on the snow-slope *above your waist,* with the pick and adze parallel to the slope. Place the rope round it and tie back to your waist in the normal way (Figure 21). If the Leader slips and slides, check the fall by gradual arrest; the axe belay will stand the diminished pull when your hands and body have taken the main shock.

The Leader advances above the belay by kicking or cutting steps and moving up in balance with his axe-point against the slope (Figure 22). Or he can plant his axe vertically while he steps on. On very steep slopes he can strike in the pick above his head to aid the move. One hard blow with the adze is better than a lot of chipping strokes in making a step; the boot consolidates the step as it is planted firmly in it, and there is no virtue in hewing great bucket-like steps. As in free rock-climbing, *balance* is the secret of safety. A good

FIG. 22

Leader will often cut one-handed and use the free hand against the slope for the balancing touch as he moves up. Speed, as well as efficiency, should be aimed at in step-cutting.

Two-handed cutting becomes necessary on very hard snow or snow-ice. You should be able to cut from either shoulder. In making a step when the surface is too hard for a slash or two to do the

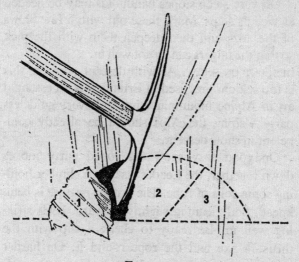

FIG. 23

job, aim at forming a step big enough to take half the boot sole; cut it beginning at the end nearest you, taking out a bit at a time (Figure 23). It should slope very slightly inwards, and the surface should not be smoothed but left rough to take the shape of the boot. Most commonly the slope is climbed on upward traverses, with larger steps cut at the turns or for belaying stances. It is important that the following climbers should use left and right feet as the Leader did and make the turns in the same way.

On very steep slopes handholds may be needed as well as steps. Mark these out with a few blows of the adze and then deepen them with the pick so that the fingers can be got well in.

DESCENT ON SNOW. As with descent on rock, this is too seldom practised in Britain; it is an essential art in Alpine mountaineering and every guideless party visiting the Alps should be already competent in snow descent.

On good easy snow the roped party moves down together, the Leader last, each climber holding some coils of rope. The proper posture is bent-kneed, body leaning slightly forward, heels striking well in. Be ready to check a slip with the thrust-in axe and the rope round it. On harder and steeper snow where downward step-cutting is necessary use the axe as anchor-belay and move one at a time. Unless the formation of the slope demands it, there is no need to descend in zigzags. The first man, belayed from above, cuts straight down, standing sideways to the slope and using the outer arm; the hand of the inner arm is used for balancing touches against the slope. Make the steps to take the side of the boot. Cut two steps, one below the other, then move the outer foot down into the lower step and the inner to the step above it; then repeat (Figure 24). To change the

FIG. 24

cutting arm, a large step is cut for the turn to the other side.

*Glissading*

Descent by sliding down a long snow-slope is only to be done if you are *sure* that the slope runs out safely, has no sudden drop or concealed rocks (these would be invisible from above), and is all continuous snow—no ice. In British gullies and couloirs especially, the good snow at the top may change without warning to ice halfway down, and there is then no hope of keeping control of your slide. For glissading you hold the axe point-downwards at your side, one hand on the head and the other on the shaft, to act as brake if necessary. Feet and knees point straight downwards, boots a little apart, body slightly crouched. There is no more exhilarating form of descent, but every year there are instances of ill-judged glissades ending fatally.

It has been said that a climber should only glissade a slope he has previously climbed up that day. But the condition of the slope can change between morning and evening.

When in any doubt, *climb* down—don't glissade.

*British Ice-climbing*

The typical British ice climb is in a gully, and the angle of the ice will be sixty degrees or more. The routes commonly demand a high degree of strength and endurance as well as special skill and special equipment. This form of ascent is

comparable in standard to advanced rock-climbing plus a certain amount of Artificial.

EQUIPMENT. Because of the high angles encountered, an ordinary ice-axe is extremely awkward

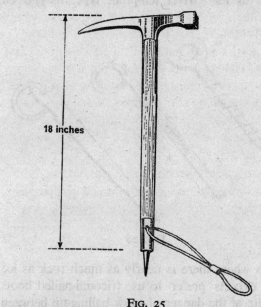

18 inches

FIG. 25

to use. The short *Hammer Axe* (Figure 25) is the
tool of the British ice-climber. The hammer end
is for driving in *ice-pitons* (Figure 26 B and C)
which may form the only available anchor belay
and are also used for direct aid, with the rope

clipped into a krab on the piton, in the manner of Artificial. For this purpose, however, the *ice-screw* (Figure 26A) is considered safer. Crampons are worn, either twelve-point ice-claws with short points or the Grivel ten-point type, though on

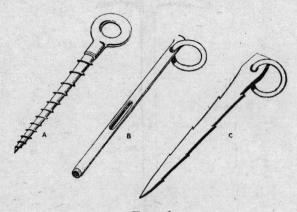

FIG. 26

routes where there is nearly as much rock as ice some experts prefer to use tricouni-nailed boots in spite of the danger of snow balling-up between the tricounis. Slings are used freely, especially for attachment to pitons while cutting steps, and several should be carried. The rope is used for belaying in the normal manner.

TECHNIQUE on British ice routes is largely a mat-

ter of repeated practice after a thorough gradua-
tion on hard steep snow; it may take several seasons to acquire. The short winter day in Britain,
and the necessary slowness of progress, make
resistance to cold an essential for the ice-climber
as well as skill and nerve.

# 5

# Alpine Mountaineering

*Approach*

Traditionally, the Alps have always been regarded by British climbers as the opportunity for exercising the craft of climbing in all its branches. The skills acquired in British hills are demanded to the full and in extended form; and besides these, new skills are needed—crampon technique and glacier craft.

The additional technique is not hard to learn. But in approaching Alpine mountaineering it is essential to know and understand the difference between this form of climbing and the sort of climbing you have learned to practise competently in North Wales or the Lakes or Scotland. The difference results from the greater height and scale of the peaks, and it affects nearly all the aspects of climbing to which British climbers are accustomed at home. The mountain surfaces are more variable, bad weather can have far more serious consequences, good route-finding becomes of vital importance. Above all, time has a new and critical significance.

The quickest and safest way to become competent in Alpine mountaineering is to do your first Alpine climbs with a guide, or to join an Alpine climbing course. The disadvantage of hiring a guide is that you lose the sense of adventure and exploration which is one of the chief pleasures of climbing. If you start Alpine climbing guideless, you retain this sense; but there is no doubt that you pay for it by taking increased risks. With this in mind, and remembering the differences that will be emphasised in the paragraphs that follow, it may be said that an experienced moderate climber with two or three companions of like standard could reasonably take a guideless climbing holiday for his first season in the Alps—provided that he chooses his district and his routes with care and common sense. By 'moderate climber' is meant one capable of leading a long climb of Very Difficult grade, experienced in British snow-climbing, accustomed to climbing in foul weather as well as in fair. As an Alpine district for a first guideless essay, he would choose the Tarentaise or Saas Fée or Arolla rather than Zermatt or Chamonix; more safely still, he could make a high-level tour, hut-to-hut, in the Oetztal or Stubai regions of the Austrian Tyrol.

On the easier peaks of the Tyrol the equipment already noted for British winter climbing will be sufficient. Almost anywhere else in the Alps, and of course on the ascent of any big peak, you must have crampons and be practised in their use.

*Crampons*

These, more than any other item of modern equipment, have changed the technique of Alpine ascent. Hard-frozen slopes where long and fatiguing periods of step-cutting slowed up earlier climbers can now be climbed in a fraction of the time with crampons. The technique of axe and crampon has replaced the old two-handed swing of the ice-axe. If you go out to climb with a guide he will certainly insist that you have crampons.

It is best to get your crampons before leaving Britain. Lightweight crampons with ten points and two forward prongs—'cow-catchers'—are the sort to buy, and the Grivel type is a good one. Have them fitted to your climbing boot and equipped with quick-release straps—and practise whenever you can find ice or hard snow. Walking on frozen surface of varying angle is the best training. The art lies in a deliberate, rhythmic placing of the boot so that all the sole spikes bite; on a steep slope the ankle is flexed for this. On very steep slopes steps may have to be cut for the crampons so that the body can stand erect above the flexed ankle. The axe can be used walking-stick fashion in cramponing up easy slopes, and on moderately steep slopes is held as shown in Figure 22. On ice or *névé* (hard-frozen upper snow) at a high angle, hold for the upward step is obtained by striking in the pick of the axe at shoulder-level. By far the most common use of crampons is on the moderate slopes of the ordinary Alpine routes where these are too hard or steep to be walked up or kicked up in vibs, and where step-cutting would take too much time.

## Other Alpine Equipment

Crampons, by virtue of their importance, have been treated separately. Moulded-rubber soles— never nailed boots—are standard Alpine wear, with crampons adding the necessary hard bite for ice or frozen snow. For the rest, equipment as for British winter climbing is used, with a few small but important additions.

SNOW-GLASSES are an absolute essential, and should always be worn on snow even though the sky is overcast. Adequate lightweight goggles can be bought cheaply in most Alpine centres; a good pair of sun-glasses, secured round the head with elastic, are almost as good. Clip-on tinted lenses can be used by those who wear spectacles.

SUN LOTION is equally essential in similar circumstances. As in the case of snow-glasses, it should be put on whenever the route lies over snow; mist or cloud merely diffuses the damaging rays, and since these rays are reflected upwards from the white surface be sure to apply lotion to the underside of exposed surfaces, such as the nostrils.

ABSEIL LINE AND LOOPS. Besides the normal equipment of two or three slings and krabs, an Alpine party should take a 100-foot abseil rope, which can be of Grade 2 nylon, and each man should have a hemp stirrup-loop for use as described later under GLACIERS.

GLOVES should be woollen—wool is excellent for the balance touches in climbing ice or iced rock—but *with* an over-mitt, preferably a proofed canvas gauntlet. Leather mitts are less suitable and are a nuisance when soaked.

CLOTHING needs a little more thought than with British climbing. Extreme heat may have to be borne while freezing cold remains a possibility. Light loose underclothing that allows the air to circulate, braces instead of belt—these are two points that help to balance the awkward extremes. A brimmed hat is favoured by some climbers; but the protective helmet, resembling a motor-cyclist's crash-helmet, is rightly becoming standard Alpine

## LEADER'S BELAY

The shoulder belay is being correctly used, with an anchor belay employing Tarbuck and Figure-of-Eight knots. Note the position of the left-hand fingers.

## SECOND'S BELAY

The waist belay is the soundest so far devised for arresting a leader's fall. Gloves are used to prevent rope burns. Notice that the Second's whole attention is fixed on the Leader.

### RUNNING BELAY

This is on Spiral Stairs route, a Very Difficult climb in Llanberis Pass, North Wales. The Leader has protected himself by placing a sling over a projection. The rope runs through the krab on the sling.

### HAND-JAMMING

To obtain hold in this smooth crack on a Yorkshire limestone cliff, the Leader uses opposing pressures of fingers and wrists. (Note, by way of warning, the very dubious state of his 'Tarbuck' knot!)

## ON TERRACE WALL VARIANT (1)

With the Third Man watching his rope, the Second makes a long step on the traverse. The climb is on the East Face of Tryfan, North Wales.

## ON TERRACE WALL VARIANT (2)

The traverse completed, the Second ascends delicately up Bollard Slab. This exposed route (Very Difficult) was first climbed in 1899 by O. G. Jones and the brothers Abraham.

*Left :* ON AN
ALPINE RIDGE

The climber, safe-
guarded by a well-
placed 'runner', is on
the East Ridge of the
Lenspitze. For a ridge
of mixed rock and
snow he carries his
crampons strapped
on top of his ruck-
sack.

*Right :* TOP PITCH
OF MEDUSA WALL

A free fall on the rope
would result if the
Leader slipped on
this hard climb on
Esk Buttress. The
jerk on the Second
and his belay can
easily be imagined
from the picture.

ARTIFICIAL
CLIMBING

Standing in an étrier,
the Leader hammers
in his next peg, to
which he will attach a
krab and clip in one
of his two ropes—
red or white—ready
for hoisting. (Wilton
Quarry, near Bolton)

EXTOL ROUTE,
DOVE CRAG

The rock on this, one
of the harder British
climbs, is sounder
than it looks. The
Leader has two ropes,
red and white, and
carries a piton ham-
mer. On the holdless
groove above him he
will need them.

## NORTH FACE OF THE CIMA GRANDE

A purely Artificial climb in the Dolomites, first achieved in 1933. The protective helmet is standard wear on such routes.

## A TRAVERSE ON SHEPHERD'S CRAG

On this low-level crag in Borrowdale rubbers are accepted wear for a dry day. The Leader is climbing on a doubled full-weight rope—an unorthodox but safe procedure.

### WALL CLIMB, BOCHLWYD BUTTRESS

This 100-foot crag in Cwm Idwal, North Wales, is typical of many small rock-faces where genuine climbing, like this Severe route, can be found.

### 'GLORY ROAD'

A Very Severe route on Derbyshire limestone at Stoney Middleton. Limestone, though less sound than gritstone, gives longer and steeper routes for outcrop climbing.

wear. Falling stones are a danger more common in the Alps than in Britain.

## Alpine Mountaineering Technique

Though the techniques of rock-climbing and snow-climbing already described form the basis of Alpine climbing, they have here to be viewed in the light of a new element: Time.

Speed is of no great moment in British climbing. Even when the short winter day ends before a party has finished the ascent of Tower Ridge on snow-clad Ben Nevis there is a safe descent by the ordinary path when at last they reach the top. It is never like this in the Alps. The climbers must start at an hour, and move at a speed, that will ensure ascent *and descent* of their peak before dark. Moreover, there are objective dangers—falling stones loosened by the sun's heat, avalanches likely to fall for the same reason—which may have to be avoided by a start well before dawn and fast movement thereafter. The routes are usually longer than any British climb, and there is often the added necessity of moving up snow-covered glacier while the snow is still frozen hard enough to give good footing and provide safe bridges over hidden crevasses.

The importance of speed becomes obvious at once if you make your first Alpine climb with a guide. He will get the party away earlier than you would have thought necessary, and if you are not in good training you will not enjoy the steady unrelenting pace. He does not hurry, but will allow no waste of time. The halts come only between long bouts of continuous climbing. On the narrow rock-ridge, where British training might insist on the absolute security of an anchor belay and movement one at a time, the guide will require the party to move together and take safeguarding belays in passing—the rope looped over a convenient spike while a difficult step is made, then flicked off quickly and progress resumed at once.

This continuous movement on exposed but not very difficult places is one of the techniques in which the newcomer to the Alps will find himself lacking; practice soon develops it, but a competent party intending to tackle guideless Alpine climbing would do well to practise it in Britain first, ascending and descending the easier Moderate rock climbs moving together. Dealing with unsound rock is another Alpine technique not to be learned in Britain unless disintegrating ridges are deliberately sought out. Descent on rock, too seldom practised in Britain, will find most Alpine beginners far slower than the guide likes; he will tend to urge the rest of the party to slither down anyhow so long as they do it quickly, while he gives a tight rope from above.

Route-finding on an Alpine peak, especially finding the descent route on a traverse, is far more difficult and important than in British climbing. With a guide, of course, there is no problem. He literally knows the route backwards; and on the innumerable Alpine routes of moderate difficulty this is his chief value, for the individual obstacles encountered on such routes are—in reasonable weather—within the technical competence of an experienced British climber. In the Alps weather can deteriorate very rapidly, and the deterioration increases the hazards of the climb. Here again the guide proves his worth, using his acquired knowledge of weather-signs to decide whether the party shall go on or retreat. On glaciers, where the route may vary from season to season, week to week, or even day to day, the guide's leadership lessens risk and may save the party hours of valuable time.

GLACIERS are dealt with in Chapter Eleven. Here the procedure for a party moving on snow-covered glacier must be mentioned as an essential part of Alpine technique.

The motion of the glacier down its rocky bed causes continual opening and closing of large cracks—*crevasses*—in the ice. These are obvious when there is no snow on the glacier, hidden when there is a thick frozen layer of snow above them. In this latter case special precaution is taken by climbing parties crossing the glacier or using it as a route up their peak. It is clear that if one of the party of three roped climbers falls through into a concealed crevasse he is in a less hazardous position than if he had only one companion; the old rule that on glacier the party should consist of at least three is still a sound one.

The three climbers, then, tie on the rope with intervals of twenty to thirty feet between them. The third man carries the 100-foot abseil line coiled on top of his rucksack. To each man's waist-loop a spare krab is clipped, and each has a loop of hemp line about nine feet in circumference attached to the climbing rope within his reach—in front of Second and Third, behind the Leader, as they move in single file with the rope not quite taut between them. The slack of this stirrup-loop can be stowed in a side pocket. The loop is attached with a *Prusik knot*, the virtue of which is that it can be moved up and down the rope easily but jams tight when strain comes on it (Figure 27). The Leader, whose task it is to watch and probe for concealed crevasses as he advances, is the most likely of the three to fall through. If he does, he can disengage his loop as he dangles below the surface and use it as a stirrup, supporting his weight and so avoiding the constriction of the waist-loop which would swiftly render him unconscious. Assuming he has been held by the men above, the rescue system described in the next chapter can be put into operation with fair hope of success.

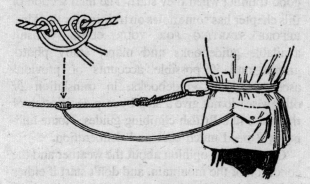

FIG. 27

### The Guideless Beginner in the Alps

Since more British climbers are nowadays making their first Alpine climbs without a guide, it will be well to summarise the procedure most likely to ensure safety and success.

BEFORE LEAVING BRITAIN—See that your party is properly constituted, its members of roughly equal competence on rock and snow. Four is a good number, climbing two on a rope on rock and all roping-up together on glacier.

Get your equipment from a reliable British supplier. Almost the only item which is cheaper abroad is the ice-axe—the Stubai axe obtainable in Austria.

See that all the members of the party are in good training when they start. The final section of this chapter has some notes on training for the Alps.

BEFORE STARTING FOR YOUR CLIMB—Consult available guidebooks and maps, study photographs and if possible accounts of previous ascents. Alpine guidebooks, in translation or otherwise, do not give a step-by-step description of the route like British climbing guides. Route-finding will need much care and deliberation.

Consult local opinion about the weather and the condition of the mountain, and don't start if either is doubtful.

Make a careful estimate of your arrival times at various points on the route, taking into consideration places which may be dangerous at certain times of day. From your estimate calculate the time you must start in order to be safely down before dark. *Then start an hour earlier than this.*

ON THE CLIMB—Keep going steadily, making long pulls and long halts (if your schedule permits them) rather than short pulls and short halts.

If the route is a plain one don't try to vary it. Divergence from the well-trodden rock ridge may land you on unsound rock.

When traversing a peak make as sure as possible of your descent route before starting to climb down.

Never hesitate to retreat when weather or route become doubtful or when one of the party shows signs of unfitness. It is bad mountaineering to go on in such cases.

Remember that accidents are most likely towards the end of a long day, when everyone is tired. At all costs resist the strong temptation to unrope on easy snow-covered glacier.

*Training for the Alps*

The basic training for Alpine mountaineering is WALKING.

Walk with crampons on snow of varying kinds whenever the opportunity serves, noting the sort of snow that balls-up in the crampon points and makes footing dangerous. In snowless seasons make long walks with a good heavy rucksack; the steeper and rougher the ground covered, the better. Walk, roped in a party, on easy ridges like Grib Goch or even Striding Edge, then practise the same continuous roped movement on easy rock climbs both in ascent and descent.

Such training is well worth while. Many climbers going out to the Alps find their first week more painful than enjoyable because they have not bothered to get into training. At the end of three weeks' climbing they will be fit and thirsting for good ascents, but by arriving well prepared for the long slogs up to the huts and the long day's effort they could have enjoyed their holiday from the beginning.

In all training aim at speed without haste, efficiency of technique without waste of time. The actions of belaying, step-cutting, using handhold and foothold, are performed hundreds of times in an Alpine day, and the saving of a few seconds in each action means the saving of perhaps an hour, with the additional safety-margin that implies, on the climb.

# 6

# Emergency and Rescue

*Approach*

It is obvious that climbing involves dangers, both subjective and objective; the possibility of a slip or error of judgement on the part of the climber, the chance of stonefall or avalanche or loose hold, are undeniably present. A great part of the attraction of mountaineering, viewed as a sport, lies in mastering the various skills that have been devised to minimise the dangers, and just as a climber takes pride in this mastery, so he should take pride in his competence to deal with all forms of mountain emergency.

One of the earliest traditions of British climbing is that when an accident occurs all mountaineers in the vicinity rally to assist in the rescue. You should be prepared to go to the help of others as well as to cope with accidents to your own party. Mountain rescue organisations exist in most European countries, and in British hills a very fine rescue system, supported by contributions from climbing clubs, operates from Mountain

Rescue Posts in the valleys, but hours must elapse before this help can reach the site of a mountain accident. The ability to give effective treatment until the rescue-party arrives is all-important, and should be acquired by everyone who goes on hills and mountains.

Emergencies not due to a serious fall or other bad injury may arise. Knowledge of how to deal with these can avert a stretcher-party or a possible fatality. They will be considered first.

*Mountain Emergencies*
BENIGHTMENT. The party becomes lost in mist or is delayed by some unforeseen incident, and is overtaken by darkness while still high up on the mountain. Much depends on whether someone in the party has knowledge of the terrain. If there is a torch available and it is decided that a known path or shelter can be reached with its aid, this can be attempted. Otherwise, the essential is to find the best possible shelter before darkness prevents safe movement. Shelter from the prevailing wind is of prime importance—the lee side of ridge or boulder, or even the building of a rough wall with rocks. As soon as movement stops, put on all available clothing and huddle close together. It is important to insulate the body from the ground as much as possible; sit on a map or guidebook if no

spare woollens can be used. If boots are wet and conditions are very cold, take off the boots and put the rucksack on over the feet. Take stock of all food and eat a little at short intervals throughout the night. As soon as it is light enough to move safely, find the way down—and be sure to report your safe arrival to anyone who may have been anxious about you.

STORM. To get quickly down into shelter is obviously the immediate aim. In a snowstorm or winter rainstorm, though, avoid the windward flank of peak or ridge. It is better to 'stay put' in good shelter on the lee side than to try to fight a way down to the valley on the exposed mountainside. In a bad thunderstorm get off summit or ridge-crest into the best possible shelter below; collect all metal equipment like krabs, pitons, and axes and stow them well away from the party. Put on all clothing and ration food in case the storm is prolonged.

EXPOSURE. Death from exposure has become increasingly frequent among mountaineers, and only recently have the dangers of this state been investigated and proper treatment devised.

Exposure can affect a climber when wind, rain, and cold act upon a body weakened by the beginning of exhaustion. If prolonged, this causes failure of the body's automatic restriction of blood-circulation, by which the temperature of the 'inner core' is maintained above danger-level; core temperature of trunk and brain drops; mental deterioration and loss of muscular co-ordination are followed by unconsciousness and death. Symptoms, any or all of which may appear, are: strange behaviour; mental lethargy; apparent partial deafness or failure of sights; stumbling and falling; sudden shivering fits. Heat loss through wind and rain towards the end of a tiring day is more likely to produce this effect than intense dry cold.

It is of prime importance to realise that the worst possible thing to do in a suspected case of exposure is to urge the victim to press on. Increased or further exertion now merely increases the rate at which cooled blood is returned to the body-core. Similarly, application of hot-water bottles, friction, or alcoholic drinks would hasten collapse and death. The best remedy is prevention—in bad weather retreat well before there is any chance of becoming exhausted. Or, if faced by blizzard or winter storm when the party is getting tired, halt in good time with some energy in reserve and use every means of conserving bodily heat in the best shelter available.

A person who has begun to suffer from exposure must be treated as a stretcher-case even if he makes some recovery and appears fit to go on.

When he has been carried to a base where further effort and heat-loss cannot take place, he can be placed in a warm bath, temperature not exceeding 113°F. This treatment is a proved life-saver.

## Mountain Accidents: Minor

CUTS AND SCRATCHES. Your chief care should be to exclude dirt from small wounds. Cover with adhesive plaster, or—in the case of larger wounds —a sterile dressing.

ROPE BURNS. These usually result from arresting a fall on the rope with bare hands. Exclude air from the burn with a clean dry dressing. Don't apply ointments or burst the blisters.

SPRAINS. Ankle-sprains are not uncommon. The important thing is to make sure it is a sprain and not a fracture; in the latter case the limb must be immobilised and the victim must await a stretcher-party. If the injury is definitely a sprain, ease the bootlaces but don't remove the boot. Apply a cold wet compress if possible; if not, bind firmly to support the limb. The injured climber can then be assisted to hobble slowly down to safety.

## Mountain Accidents: Serious

When a climber is rendered helpless by injury the rescue organisation must be put into operation at once and with care, as detailed in the next section.

Meanwhile, carry out the following procedure:
1. DIAGNOSE THE INJURIES. These may be obvious
—a broken limb or an open wound—and first aid
can be applied. If the victim is plainly badly hurt,
but the injury is not obvious, *don't attempt to
move him or apply experimental treatment;* should
the injury be internal, spinal, or to the head, you
will do much more harm than good. In all cases,
however, you *must* treat the victim for shock as
soon as possible.
2. TREAT FOR SHOCK. Use all available means to
make and keep the patient *warm.* Don't move
him more than you can help and at all costs avoid
causing more pain, but if possible get some insula-
tion, spare woollen sweaters for instance, between
him and the ground. Persons suffering from shock
are very liable to exposure, so contrive shelter
(such as a wall of stones or a tent or anoraks)
against wind or rain. Don't give drinks, but get the
victim to suck glucose tablets or sweets if he is
conscious. Be cheerful and encouraging; assure
him that rescue is at hand and that all will be well.
3. STOP BLEEDING from open wounds by bandag-
ing *gently but firmly.*
4. ATTEND TO THE VITAL FUNCTIONS, especially if
the patient is unconscious. Ensure that he can
breathe freely, loosening restricting clothes about
neck and chest and removing false teeth if worn.

If breathing is faint and heart-beat weak, apply up-and-down pressure on the patient's breast-bone at the rate of about sixty times in a minute until the heart-beat strengthens. It is no good dealing with broken limbs until heart and lungs are functioning normally.

5. DEAL WITH FRACTURES. Unless you are a doctor or genuinely skilled in first aid don't attempt to do more than *free the injured climber from pain*. This is the most important thing you can do and may save his life. Handle him as little as possible. If he is conscious use his guidance to find the position of the broken limb which gives him most freedom from pain; then pad it generously round the fracture and immobilise it as well as you can. Never attempt to straighten a bad fracture, but with a broken leg or hip it may be possible to immobilise the injured limb by binding it firmly to the sound leg. A broken arm is best supported across the chest with a bandage, triangular or improvised. Remember: if your efforts to help cause extra pain you are doing harm; stop at once and concentrate on finding a position that will ease pain.

6. SUSPECT SPINAL INJURY in all cases of fall from a height. Inability of the victim to move his limbs will be a sufficient reason for diagnosing injury to the spine. In this case *don't move the patient*

*at all*. Treat for shock, and make sure that the message calling out the rescue-party reports your diagnosis.

## Mountain Rescue

The Mountain Distress Signal blown on a whistle (see Chapter One) may bring other climbers to your aid. Meanwhile a message should be sent as soon as possible to the nearest Mountain Rescue Post or other source of help. Ideally, two messengers should go down together, but an injured climber must not be left alone unless the climbing-party numbered two only and there is no alternative.

The message, which should preferably be in writing, must contain the following information:

—Exact position of the casualty; either a six-figure map reference or clear instructions enabling the rescuers to make straight for the spot. If the fall has occurred on a rock climb, give the name of the cliff, the route, and the pitch where it happened.

—Time of the accident.

—Number of people injured.

—Nature of the injuries.

If two climbers are alone, and one of them is seriously injured, the uninjured man must use all spare clothing to make his companion warm and comfortable before leaving him to go for help. If he is unconscious he must be secured with the rope so that he cannot fall or roll down. If at all possible, a cheering message should be left where he will not fail to see it if he regains consciousness. The man going for help must be absolutely sure that he can inform the rescue-party *exactly* where the injured man is, or be able to guide them himself to the spot.

## Rescue from a Crevasse

Charles Evans, one of the greatest climbers of our day, has said that getting out of a crevasse is so difficult that it is worth going to almost any lengths to avoid falling into one. In considering the two methods of crevasse rescue described below this dictum should be borne in mind.

THE PARTY OF THREE OR MORE. Assuming that the party is roped together and prepared as described in Chapter Five under the heading GLACIERS, and the Leader (the most likely man) falls into a hidden crevasse, the method of getting him out—one of several—would be as follows:

1. The typical crevasse is bottle-shaped and the Leader is thus hanging free on the rope. His first action is to disengage his stirrup-loop, get his foot into it, and adjust the position of the

Prusik knot until he can stand in it and relieve the constriction of the rope.

2. The Second, above him, will have checked his fall, perhaps assisted by the Third Man. The Second drives in his axe to secure a firm anchorage and belays to it with his stirrup-loop. The Third comes forward and helps to shift the Prusik knot until the axe-stirrup belay is supporting the whole weight of the fallen man.

3. The Third drives in his own axe as firmly as possible and, uncoiling the 100-foot abseil rope, attaches one end of it securely to his axe. Then, belayed by the Second, he advances near the edge of the crevasse and lowers the bight of the doubled abseil rope to the Leader. A folded anorak is placed under the doubled rope to ease its run over the snow edge.

4. The Leader clips the abseil rope into the spare krab on his waist-loop and signals that he is ready.

5. Second and Third haul together on the free part of the abseil rope, which runs through the Leader's krab as through a pulley, while the Leader helps by pulling on the part attached to the ice-axe (see diagram, Figure 28).

This method has proved efficient when circumstances are favourable. It is said to work when there are only two on the rope and one falls through, but the hazards would obviously be greater.

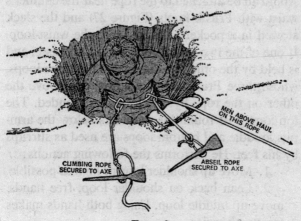

FIG. 28

## The Party of Two

The pair of climbers who are prepared to chance the extra hazards in order to maintain their partnership might consider learning, *and practising beforehand,* the Prusik self-rescue method. This method makes it possible for a man hanging free on the rope to raise himself to safety by his own efforts, and could be a life-saver on overhanging rock as well as in crevasse rescue.

Each of the two climbers carries three nine-foot

loops (two can be used successfully, but the third is invaluable in relieving the strain). Before starting across snow-covered glacier the three loops would all be attached to the rope near the climber's waist with Prusik knots (Figure 27) and the slack stowed in a pocket or tucked into the waist-loop. If one of the two falls through into a crevasse, and is held by the other, he disengages the three loops, whose three Prusik knots are now one above the other on the rope by which he is suspended. The top loop goes round his shoulders below the armpits, middle and bottom loops are used as stirrups by his feet. He performs the following actions:

1. Move up shoulder loop as high as possible.

2. Lean back on shoulder loop, free hands, move up middle loop. Using both hands makes this much easier.

3. Move up bottom loop.

4. Supporting weight on both feet in middle and bottom loops, move up shoulder loop again.

5. Repeat until top of rope is reached.

It must be emphasised again that this method demands previous practice if it is to be successful in emergency.

## Other Alpine Emergencies

FROSTBITE (not unknown in British winter climbing) reveals itself by dead whiteness and lack of all sensation in the part affected. The old remedies of rubbing—with snow or anything else—or flogging until feeling returns are dangerous and should never be applied. The best remedy on the mountain is to warm the part immediately by placing it under the armpit or other warm part of a companion's body. Immersion in warm—not very hot—liquid is better if this happens to be available. The treatment is very painful to the victim. Afterwards, cover the frostbitten area with the softest material available and bandage lightly. Hospital treatment should follow as soon as possible.

SNOW-BLINDNESS. This is often caused by not putting on snow-glasses soon enough or leaving them off for long periods. It is always very painful. The only treatment is to get the victim into a darkened room or other lightless place as soon as possible. Cocaine drops in the eye help to alleviate the pain. Failing this, bathing with a solution of salt in warm water may be effective.

# PART TWO

# Basic Theory

# 7

# Route-finding

A. F. Mummery, the great climber whose daring first ascents on the Chamonix Aiguilles at the end of last century began modern rock-climbing, wrote these words: 'The true mountaineer is a wanderer . . . a man who loves to be where no human being has been before, who delights in gripping rocks that have previously never felt the touch of human fingers.' This, from a man whose preference was for steep rock, points the fact that most climbers obtain fullest satisfaction in finding their own way rather than in following oft-repeated routes. Perhaps this applies more particularly to British climbers, for in this country the Continental custom of 'waymarking' mountain routes with coloured paint has so far not been adopted, and proposals for waymarking always meet with strong resistance.

Nowadays it is far from easy to find, in Britain, 'rocks that have previously never felt the touch of human fingers'. Almost every yard of discover-

able crag has a climbing-route across it, and real
rock-climbing discovery is practically limited to
the faces of limestone and other friable rock which
are climbable only by the newer methods of
Artificial. All the same, route-finding still plays a
part, however diminished, in every ascent of a
rock route, and adds to the pleasure of the climb.
In greater mountains it plays a much bigger part;
and in British hill-walking it will remain a necessary and important craft until all the mountain
tracks are waymarked and all the moorland routes
signposted or restricted to the following of
power-lines.

The art of steering a course by map and compass has recently become a popular sport under
the name of Orienteering. This is one of the two
related aspects of route-finding. Properly used,
the map can tell you which way to go and what
sort of obstacles lie on the route, but it cannot tell
you which route to follow in dealing with the obstacles. Picking your way on the actual terrain—
the safest, the quickest, or the easiest way—is the
second aspect of route-finding.

First, consider the map. For mountaineering
purposes the one-inch British Ordnance Survey
map is the best, because it combines a sufficiency
of detail with a wide coverage of terrain that enables distant peaks to be used for taking bearings

and establishing position. The Siegfried maps of
the Alps and the Swiss *Landeskarte*, both on a
scale of 1 : 50,000 (roughly 1¼ inches to the mile),
are the best for the same reason. The 2½-inch
maps of the British Ordnance Survey are useful
for detailed exploration of a small area, but add
little information of use to the mountaineer, while
the six-inch sheets are useful only to such special-
ists as the geologist and antiquarian. The half-inch
maps are handy for planning a tour, but are too
lacking in detail for safe use in mountain country.

The British one- inch maps whose use was
briefly described in Chapter One are imprinted
with the lines of the National Grid running north-
south and east-west, the squares enclosing one
square kilometre. Since a curved surface is here
represented as flat, the north-south lines do not
run *exactly* True north and south, but the variation is so slight that it need not be taken into account in ordinary compass work. Each grid line
is numbered, and this enables any point on the
map to be identified by a grid reference accurate
to 100 metres. The vertical lines (numbered at
top and bottom of the map sheet) are used first
to find the east-west square in which the object
lies, estimating its position across the square in
tenths; if it lay halfway between north-south lines
64 and 65 this part of the reference would be 645.

The object is pinpointed by similarly estimating its position between the horizontal lines. Thus the full grid reference of the summit of Snowdon could be given as: O.S. Sheet 107, 609543. The importance of being able to give an exact position in this way was emphasised in Chapter Six.

In describing compass work the variation between True North and Magnetic North was mentioned. The variation differs in different parts of the world and is continually changing, though very slowly. At the foot of the map you will find exact information about this. For instance, the 1962 edition of O.S. Sheet 197 bears these words: 'Mag North *about 8°W. in 1962 decreasing by about ½° in six years.*' Until 1976 or thereabouts we can take the variation as 8°W. as was done in the example given in Chapter One; after that we shall get the compass needle pointing 7°W. of North when setting the map. But for work of such accuracy, perhaps using a prismatic compass, you would also take into account the grid variation which is given on all one-inch Ordnance maps. Sheet 107, for instance, states that in the N.W. corner of the map True North is 1° 50'E. of the direction indicated by the vertical grid lines; so for real accuracy in laying-off a course on this part of the map you would get the north-south axis of your compass pointing about

2°E. of the grid-line direction before turning map and compass together until the needle points 8°W. of north.

Cross-bearings have been mentioned as a way of fixing position. To do this you need to have two clear distant objects that you can identify on the map, such as mountain peaks, and these should lie, if possible, on lines making a right-angle at your position. Holding the compass with its needle pointing 8°W. of north, sight across its dial and note where the line from you to Object A cuts the edge of the dial—it could be, say, at the figure 95. The True Bearing of Object A, then, is 95°. Next, sight in the same way on Object B, whose True Bearing may turn out to be 220°. Since these figures are the bearings of the peaks from your unknown position from the peaks—the 'back-bearings'. To do this, relate them to 180— adding if the total will not come to more than 360, subtracting if it is greater. Back-bearing A will be 275°, back-bearing B will be 40°. Now spread the map and place the compass with its centre over Object A and the N on the dial aligned with map north. The needle can be ignored. Draw with a pencil a straight line through Object A and the figure 275 on the dial. Then, with the compass centre exactly over Object B, draw a line through Object B and the figure 40 on the dial. Where these lines cross is your position on the map.

This method of finding position is called 'taking a fix', and it can be made more accurate if a third object is used to give an additional back-bearing. A slight inaccuracy in sighting may cause the three lines to make a triangle where they cut (the 'triangle of error') and in this case your position lies somewhere inside the triangle. With a prismatic compass a fix can be taken with much greater accuracy than an ordinary compass will give, but a rough fix by sighting with a dial-type compass can often be useful.

In using the compass it is important to remember that metal objects, or exposure meters, can affect the compass needle if they are near it. In certain places (the Main Ridge of the Coolin in Skye is a notable example) the compass is unreliable because of magnetic attraction in the rocks.

It was said in Chapter One that the making of a time-distance schedule before setting out on a mountain expedition was an excellent plan. This is especially true of Alpine mountaineering and for leaders of youth parties in British hills. By way of example, here is a time-distance schedule for the crossing of Scafell Pike from Wastdale Head to the Dungeon Ghyll Hotel in Langdale. Naismith's Rule (see Chapter One) is used.

|  | *Time* |
|---|---|
| Leave Wastdale Head | 0930 |
| Lane S.S.W. to bridge over stream and cart-track heading S.E.; gain *foot of Lingmell Gill*. 1½ m., no climbing | 1000 |
| E. up Lingmell Gill to col between Lingmell Crag and Scafell Pike, then S.S.E. to *summit of Pike*. 2 m., 3,000 ft. | 1220 |
| Allow 1 hour for rests and lunch. Leave summit of Scafell Pike | 1320 |
| Descend N.E. from summit, continue N.E. 1 m. including up-and-down over Broad Crag to *saddle just S. of Great End* | 1345 |
| Due E. (first a traverse then descent) for ½ m. from saddle to reach Esk Hause; from Esk Hause steer E.S.E. ¾ m. over intermediate height to *Angle Tarn* | 1415 |
| From the S. end of the tarn go on E.S.E. (slight ascent) to strike the gap between Hanging Knotts and Rossett Pike, ¼ m. Descend very steeply, E.S.E. and then E., by Rossert Gill to join *track coming down from Stake Pass;* 1 m. | 1450 |
| Continue S.E. down the head of Langdale by good track to reach *Hotel*, 2 m. | 1530 |

Time, allowing 1 hour for lunch halt only, 6 hours
Map-distance 9½ miles

Notice that short time-distance estimates have been made for the descent, where the course is changed quite often. This gives an additional check in thick mist. Note also that to cover a map-distance of nine and a half miles takes—by this estimate—five hours of actual steady going. Foot-paths are marked on the map for most of this route, but it is wise to check the route by your schedule as if the paths were not there, though you would of course use them; many a party has lost itself in mist through going on along a path from which they should have diverged. Moreover, many mountain paths are by no means as obvious as the map leads you to think.

When compass-work has been mastered, the map studied, and the day's climb scheduled and checked, the second aspect of route-finding makes its demand as soon as you set foot on the mountain. Unless there is a beaten track all the way, a route must be found up grass and scree and rock, round one side or the other of obstacles, across or round bog. A party of experienced mountaineers always walks in single file on rough pathless terrain. This is not arbitrary convention, but plain common sense. On such ground there is only one 'best way', and the man most capable of selecting it goes first, with his companions making comfortable use of his skill. A good Leader will often take his party up a very steep and rough mountainside so easily that they feel he has been using a path.

The secret of this useful art lies in foresight. The Leader, at a first swift glance, sees the 'line of weakness' on the broken slope or up the easy rocks and follows it with his eye to register it on his memory. This gives him the general route to follow, and when he comes to move up its details he is again looking ahead, planning the places higher up where he will set his feet and arranging his nearer steps to bring him easily to those places. In more detail still, he looks for and uses the best foothold—flat ledges instead of slanting, short upward steps instead of long ones. He has in mind the dictum of that great and tireless climber Geoffrey Winthrop Young: *The effort you put into each step should be the same, whatever the change in the angle of the surface.* With practice and experience this pre-selection of the way becomes automatic, and it can make all the difference between exhaustion and freshness at the end of the trek. In the Alps it can mean the difference between safety and danger.

The single-file rule should be broken when a party is ascending or descending a screeslope. The man or men above can hardly avoid dislodging stones which might injure those lower down. On scree, therefore, move in echelon or arrowhead formation, keeping fairly close together.

Bogs and marshes are almost a specialist's delight when it comes to crossing them. If a simple detour cannot be made round the boggy area, pick the driest route across by observing where the tufts of vegetation grow closest together. On

British mountains there are very few bogs, if any, where a man could sink dangerously deep or get stuck fast; but any flat patches of pale bright green should be avoided.

Take no chances with streams in flood after heavy rain. Rather than try to boulder-hop on the brink of a fall, take off boots and wade across higher up. Highland burns are especially liable to rise in spate during a wet day, and can become literally impossible to cross without risk. The river bank in a long boggy glen often gives the best going. But it is *not* safe, if you get lost in mist, to find the nearest stream and follow it down; as often as not, the way of the water is the steepest way, and may be a plunge down an impassable chasm. Innumerable Highland streams give plain proof of this.

If you are following an undulating ridge in mist, don't be tempted to short-cut its humps by contouring on a flank unless the crest becomes too narrow and difficult. It is very easy to miss the next gap, lose height imperceptibly, and lose yourself among the screes and crags of the flank. The following of the crest itself is not always perfectly simple in mist. Spurs and side ridges, often ending in steep crags, branch from the crest and a careless mountaineer can stray on to one of these without knowing it. The obvious safeguard is to know,

from the map, the direction of the main crest and
check frequently with the compass that you are
still going in that direction.

Route-finding on the grand scale—finding a way
up an unexplored mountainside—is really impossible in Britain and the Alps. But something like
it can be managed artificially in the remoter Highlands, and a guideless party in the Alps will
quite possibly find themselves faced with the
necessity of dealing with an ascent or descent not
allowed for in their programme. When information obtained from mountains by the eye alone
has to be converted into a practicable route there
are some facts that are worth remembering.

It is extremely difficult to judge the angle of a
rock-face or snow-slope when looking at it from
directly in front, especially if your angle of sight
is upward. Generally, the rock-face appears
steeper than it really is; it always looks less
broken than it is. Lliwedd, the big rock-face on
Snowdon in North Wales, looks like a thousand-
foot wall of sheer slabs when you view it from the
shore of the lake at its foot. Looking down from
the top of the rock-face, you see innumerable
ledges criss-crossing the wall—apparently providing easy ways down everywhere. Both impressions
are wrong. A front view of a long ascending ridge
will persuade you that it is very steep and quite

continuous, whereas you can safely assume that it is broken into steps and that the angle is at any rate considerably less than your eye tells you. Similarly, the great flank of snow opposite you will look fearfully steep, if not vertical; but common sense must declare that snow could not possibly lie at that angle and that the slope is climbable if in good condition.

Scale is one of the most difficult things to judge in mountains where there are no objects of known size, like stone walls or sheep, to correct the eye. Even in British hills many a hopeful rock climber has toiled up the scree to a line of crags, thinking to make new routes on a hitherto untouched 200-foot cliff, only to find his fine precipice a mere fifty-foot escarpment. Distances are hard to estimate by eye, in the same way; and the particular lighting of the day or season can make far objectives look near or send a summit, really only ten minutes' scramble above us, into a hazy distance that suggests an hour of toil to gain it.

The map can correct this human fallibility. But only long experience—the store of remembered mistakes and triumphs—can teach the climber to judge accurately, in the face of the actual problem, the safe way up a trackless mountain-flank or the virgin rock-route that will 'go'.

# 8

# The Climbing Rope

A favourite aphorism of mountaineering savants
half a century ago was: 'The climbing rope is used
for moral support only'. A later comment on this
was expressed in verse:

> 'According to some schools of thought
> The rope is "moral" in support;
> But should the climber fall, the rope
> Affords him some (immoral) hope.'

Today—setting aside the direct-aid system of
Artificial—the rope in free-climbing is still considered rather as a safeguard than as an aid, and to
receive any physical assistance from it, such as a
pull-up for the Second or a top rope lowered
from above to the Leader, is interpreted as a con-
fession of failure. All the same, the old-timers'
tendency to treat their linking rope as a sort of
spiritual encouragement instead of as the vital
safety-factor in mountaineering has gone. In place
of those frighteningly casual belay methods illu-

strated in the climbing photos of the 'twenties a safeguarding system as mechanically sound as possible is used, and for the hard move at the end of a long run-out (which the pioneers regarded as a test of nerve) the Leader does not hesitate to protect himself with a sling and running-belay.

The nature of the rope has changed since those early days. The natural-fibre rope, hemp, still has its uses, particularly as waist lengths and abseil belay slings. For the climbing rope nylon has superseded hemp. A hawser-laid rope, each strand consisting of many thousands of nylon filaments, has the great advantage of extra tensile strength— a 100-foot length will stretch under strain to 110 feet before breaking—and is not subject to deterioration like natural fibre. It has one major fault, its low melting-point, which makes it liable to failure if overheated by great friction; and a minor one, that it is smoother than hemp and less easy to grip. The ideal rope for climbing has yet to be produced, but in spite of later productions from polythene, perlon, and polypropylene, and the popularity of the perlon kernmantel rope, hawser-laid nylon rope is so far the best for use in free rock-climbing.

British Standard 3104 was compiled to establish the minimum requirements of a safe climbing rope, and the heaviest of the nylon ropes, Grade

4, conforms to these. Here are the particulars of the four grades of nylon rope:

| Grade | Weight in lb. per 100 feet | Circumference in. | Minimum Breaking Load lb. |
|---|---|---|---|
| 4 | 5·5 | 1⅜ | 4,200 |
| 3 | 4·25 | 1¼ | 3,500 |
| 2 | 2·5 | ⅞ | 2,000 |
| 1 | 1·25 | ⅝ | 1,000 |

The circumstances in which a rope may be put to its severest test in climbing are so various that tests to provide for them all are difficult to devise. It is well known that if a knot is used to secure the rope to the climber the rope is markedly weaker at the knot than anywhere else; yet in the few cases where the rope has broken under a fall it has never broken at the knot. On several occasions it has been the severing of the strands over a rough edge that has caused the break, and for this reason some climbers prefer to climb on two ropes of Grade 3 rather than a single rope of Grade 4, arguing that the severing of both ropes by abrasion is very unlikely.

The *kernmantel* rope has special merits in Artificial. Its straight perlon filaments are enclosed in a braided sheath, which allows it to run through karabiners under tension more easily than a hawser-laid rope. The sheath also protects against abrasion to some extent. However, the *kernmantel* under strain is less flexible than Grade 4 nylon, and its extensibility is much less. It is also heavier and thicker, the sheath contributing nothing to its strength.

The point of vital importance about nylon rope has already been mentioned: the generation of heat by friction in its use must be avoided. Nylon must never have the chance of chafing against nylon, which much increases the possibility of damage by heat; waist lengths and other cordage with which the moving rope could come into contact are therefore of hemp. Similarly, the use of special abseil gadgets of metal (*descendeurs*) or abseiling with the nylon rope running round a karabiner in two or three turns are best avoided. Long Alpine abseils by one or other of these methods have been known to damage the rope. Apart from this danger, the resistance of nylon to damp and rot inclines many climbers to assume that it is everlasting and needs no attention. This is far from being the case. A nylon rope can become seriously damaged without revealing it to a cursory glance, and since it is the climber's life insurance it should be examined regularly and discarded if found to be faulty.

Examination should be done foot by foot, in daylight. Look for the following:

External wear caused by dragging over rough surfaces or running loaded through karabiners; a flattening of the outside of the strands reveals this. The 'fluffiness' of the surface only indicates normal wear.

Bad abrasion of a strand—many torn filaments showing their ends. Tension over a sharp edge can cause this.

Internal wear; if the strands part easily, or loose fibres can be pulled out, this is present. It can be caused by particles of grit getting between the strands—as from dragging the rope carelessly on wet glacier.

Chemical attack; shown by surface softening or weakening locally so that fibres can be rubbed or pulled off.

Heat damage; this may be fairly obvious—the fusing of the fibres making a hard glazed skin, or beads or globules of melted nylon, but it can also be difficult to detect. If a nylon rope is known to have been subjected to violent friction, such as a leader's fall may cause, it should not be used for rock-climbing again.

In using the rope on a mountain, don't tread on it, even in vibs, and see that nobody else does. Avoid dragging it over rock, snow, or ice. Keep it clean from mud and grit as far as possible.

After using it, store it in a dry airy place away from strong light. If it has been badly soiled, rinse it first in clean water. Never dry it by heat or in hot sunshine. Be sure it is not placed or stored near battery acid, creosote, carbolic acid, lysol, or other acids and alkalis. Even at the cost of appearing selfish, don't lend the rope to other climbers.

Where hemp is concerned the danger of rot and mildew is far greater. Even when a hemp waist length has not been subjected to a great deal of wetting and drying it is wisest to discard it after six months' use and get a new one.

*A safeguarding system as mechanically sound as possible* was the phrase used at the beginning of this chapter to describe the purpose of the climbing rope. To be 'mechanically sound' the system must use to the full the strength and resilience of the climber's body as well as that of the rope; hence the shoulder belay (Chapter Two) though quite good enough for supporting a man directly below, is faulty and even dangerous in trying to arrest a fall from above, because the strain will come on a framework of bone and joint inadequate to stand it. The waist belay, which contrives that the shock will come on the much stronger framework of hip and leg, has been described in Chapter Two. The method was devised by Kenneth Tarbuck (who invented his autonomous knot) and is known as the Tarbuck friction-arrest belay. Some additional points about it should be noted.

The essence of good belaying by the Second is preparedness. Preparedness consists, first, of devoting the whole of your attention to the Leader's movements and, second, calculating at each stage of his progress where and how the shock will come if he falls off. As Second belaying the Leader, you will stand on your ledge or footholds facing outwards from the rock-face, because if you faced inwards a fall would drag the rope from its checking slide round your waist above the hip bones. It is usually possible to turn the upper body so as to observe the Leader's movements above. If he is a little to your left overhead as you face outwards, the left arm and hand control the rope running up to him; the right arm, with one turn of the rope round the sleeve, handles the slack as it runs out to his ascent. Reverse this if he is above you to your right. Anticipate a possible fall, taking into account your own and the Leader's position and the formation of the cliff below. If the fall happens, coming from above on your left, brace the body with knees slightly bent and the left leg ready to take strain; bring the left hand across the body close to the right; tighten the grip of the right (gloved) hand, using this and the forearm turns, with the friction round the waist, to take the shock of the pull and begin the arrest; finally tighten the

(gloved) left hand to complete the arrest. The anchor belay must always be tight to your waist
length, never slack, for a friction-arrest belay.

It will be obvious that nothing but actual practice can give confidence in using this belay. Many
climbing clubs organise an annual 'Falling Meet',
using an eleven-stone dummy (such as a sack of
sand) which is pushed off the crag from above the
Second, and every climber should make a special
point of getting the invaluable experience such
simulated accidents provide.

The friction-arrest waist belay described above
and in Chapter Two follows the methods now
being taught at the centres of climbing instruction
in Britain. It may be that actual experience of the
method will lead you to modify some of the points
to suit your personal requirements. There is no
point in sticking to a rigid procedure if you find
you have a better chance of saving the Leader by
using hand or body in a slightly different manner.
For instance, an expert climber who has experienced more than a hundred simulated falls, holding them with the friction-arrest belay, has educed
from his experience the following points, some of
which differ from accepted method:

The shoulder belay is not only inefficient in
holding a falling Leader but also capable of causing severe injury to the Second.

The friction by which the main arrest is made should be caused by the degree of 'wrap' across the body rather than by the grasp of the hands; there is no need to wear gloves, or to take a turn of the rope round the braking arm, which can be deprived of control by the excessive friction.

On a fall occurring, the hand nearest the Leader is brought to a position that makes the line of fall, the belayer's body, and the anchor belay behind him into one straight line. At the same time the other hand is swept right across the body until the rope it is grasping overlaps the rope going down to the falling man. This 360 degree wrap round the body provides the maximum friction that can be applied.

The Leader-side hand should let the rope slide freely and is not used in holding the fall. The braking hand is not tightened until the body-friction has absorbed the initial shock; then it closes with quickly increasing firmness.

The legs should be kept straight, feet about twenty-four inches apart, straddled across the line of expected fall.

The braking arm (away from the Leader) should be kept straight and rigid so that it is not pulled behind the body.

The waist belay round the Second's body develops maximum friction when the Leader has fallen about fifteen feet. No fall, however great, of more than this distance will increase the pressure or jerk on the Second's body.

The slack of the rope should be lying below the braking hand in irregular loose coils—not in a neat tight coil—so that it runs from the top of the coil and not from underneath it.

The multiple hemp waist length with large screw-gate karabiner, used with the Tarbuck knot and the rope as tight as possible to the anchor-point, is by far the best form of anchor belay.

In these findings the two main differences from the accepted Tarbuck method for friction arrest are that no turn of the rope is taken round the forearm and that gloves are considered unnecessary. It is suggested that unless and until you have experienced several test falls you should use gloves when belaying the Leader and retain the rope-turn round the braking arm, as instructed in Chapter Two.

A good Second does more than merely adjust body and rope according to the way he has been taught. Every stance, every pitch, every possible line of fall, is different, and he must adjust himself mentally as well as physically to each change of circumstance when he reaches a stance. During the Leader's ascent of the pitch, too, conditions may change. For instance, when the Leader decides to use a running belay the direction of pull in the event of his fall (as already mentioned) will change—it will haul the Second upwards instead of downwards. But the Second, providing as well as he can for this possibility, must also consider the possibility of the runner failing; if the Leader has had to use a line sling and his route above it is steep and hard, this could happen. The Second has then to be prepared for both kinds of pull. Leader and Second together should try to foresee the use of a runner before the Leader starts to climb the pitch, and contrive the anchor belay accordingly. Two belays, one for an upward pull and one for a downward, are seldom found on a stance, and the thread belay is the only one which will withstand both pulls. Sometimes the only way out of the quandary is a piton, driven well in with a piton hammer.

If the Leader is conscious and unhurt after an arrested fall it may be possible to lower him to the stance below, or he may be able to climb up to the Second. If he is injured or unconscious, circumstances will determine the Second's actions. The Mountain Distress Signal (page 112) will be used to summon help. If help is unlikely to arrive, the Second will have to secure the Leader's rope to the belay, detach himself, and either finish the climb unroped and go for help or descend to try to help the Leader. Both procedures are bound to be hazardous. Obviously a party of three would be in a far stronger position to deal with such an emergency.

The Leader's capability of leading a difficult climb safely depends in large degree on the trust he can repose in his Second. And by way of this we return to the traditional theory of the rope's value as a moral support. A century ago, long before the technique of the climbing rope had been evolved and when many climbers still regarded it as a rather futile precaution, Edward Whymper commented on his roped party as follows: 'The certainty and safety of the method gave confidence to the man who was moving, and not only nerved him to put out his powers to the utmost, but sustained nerve in really difficult situations.' With sound belaying this confidence is justified, and it is the real secret of a good Leader's success. In fact, Leader and Second form a team, and a novice or a feeble Second on the rope behind him will prevent the Leader from using his climbing skill to the full. Dr. Charles Evans has said: 'To be slovenly in the management of the rope is not a mark of courage, but of negligence and stupidity.' The mental attitude that says: 'It's very unlikely that X will fall in leading this pitch, so I needn't give him much of a belay' is to be condemned very strongly. More often than not, a fall takes place when it is least expected, especially when the main difficulties and tensions of the route are past. On more than one occasion a fatal fall has occurred from comparatively easy ground after the party has unroped.

If the strength of a climbing rope depends on the way it is used as much as on its material and construction, the strength of a 'rope' of climbers depends on the collective skill and care of the whole party. It has often been remarked that the connecting fibres seem to convey the confidence or lack of confidence of one man to another, and experience confirms this. Indeed, it can reasonably be maintained that three good climbers on one are a stronger party than two. Modern practice prefers the rope of two, and where speed is important two climbers on a rope are certainly twice as fast as three; but anyone who has climbed with two trusted companions of roughly his own competence will know the quite surprising access of confidence that comes from the extra man on the rope. And this does not stem entirely from the knowledge that in accident or emergency there will be more helpers. It does appear that the sum of the skill and cheerfulness behind him passes up the rope to help the Leader—that the 'spiritual link' perceived by the pioneers has a basis in fact.

# 9

## Weather and Equipment

In *Mountain Craft* Geoffrey Winthrop wrote: 'The weather is the background, foreground, and middle distance of all big mountaineering. . . . Every mountaineer keeps one eye on this irresponsible neutral, which may at any time turn the scale of the campaign against him.' Climbing technique may have changed since the day when *Mountain Craft* was published, but the character of mountain weather has not. It remains the 'irresponsible' neutral' that interferes continually in the amicable contest between man and mountain, often with the effect of turning the day's pleasure into a struggle for life.

This is not only the case in what Winthrop Young terms 'big mountaineering'—Alpine climbing and ascents in greater ranges—though in such climbing the penalties of being caught high up by bad weather are more severe. In British hills the onset of storm or cold rain can be just as sudden and unexpected, and while the descent to safety is shorter and easier than it would be in the Alps, the climbers on Crib Goch or Helvellyn are likely to be less experienced than those you would find on a ridge of the Dent Blanche or the Meije. The primary defence against bad weather on mountains is to come down to, or not to start up from, the valley. It was pointed out in Chapter One that 'bashing on' through rain or snow on a valley road is a totally different matter from 'bashing on' with a mountain climb in similar conditions. In fact, the conditions will not be similar, because the factors that merely bring discomfort in the valley—cold, wet, high wind, poor visibility—are all intensified to danger-point on a mountain. In Britain the tendency of many climbers to ignore bad weather is due to two things: a mistaken idea that the home mountains are so easy that bad weather makes little or no difference, and the natural desire to make the most of a short weekend in the hills. A high proportion of fatalities (and many more narrow escapes) would have been avoided if the victims had joined moral courage to ordinary prudence and cancelled or modified the day's climbing programme in view of the weather. This is simple enough when the weather is already bad before the start is to be made. It is less simple to forecast a weather-change when the morning is fair or merely doubtful, but all climbers and mountain-walkers should have at least a rudimentary idea of how to do it.

Whether in Britain or the Alps, the area forecast on the radio is a useful general guide. However, it has to be taken in conjunction with the familiar saying that 'mountains make their own weather', especially in the Alps where big isolated mountains may brew storms on their summits when the lower slopes are in sunlit calm. It is well known that in small mountain areas like North Wales or the Lake District the weather may be foul on one side of the district and fair and dry on the other; the area forecasts are not able to predict such differences, within a few miles of each other. Next to the area forecast, the barometer is the thing to consult—not, of course, by the position of its indicator needle but by the direction and speed of its movement. A rapid fall probably means the swift approach of bad weather which will not last for long, and similarly a rapid rise indicates good weather for a short period. A slow steady fall marks the slow approach of worsening weather, but at the beginning of such a fall you can usually assume that for some hours, perhaps for the whole day, there will be no great change.

In unfamiliar districts it is advisable to consult the local wiseacres about the weather to be expected. There is really no substitute for experience in judging weather portents, and if you can get an honest opinion from a farmer or peasant who has lived all his life among those particular mountains it can be immensely useful. In every mountain district the weather signs are different—one might say in every mountain valley—and the signs you have learned to interpret in Wasdale will not do for forecasting the day's weather at Zermatt. With this warning in mind, there are some visual indications that can give at least a probability.

Clouds are a handy short-term indication. If they maintain their shape, rain is still unlikely; if they alter without growing less, a change for the worse is imminent. Cumulus clouds give the best indication, by towering and breaking at the top for rain or by shrinking and thinning out for better weather. High cirrus clouds mean rain. If either cirrus or cumulus begins to stretch out into long stratified bands at any height it heralds the approach of bad weather. The 'anvil shape' of a thunder-cloud is well known, and it must be remembered that in the Alps thunder on a peak always means snow and intensified cold. Hard-outlined clouds mean wind high up, long cloud-fingers radiating from a peak mean storm.

The wind can give a longer-term forecast. In Britain we know that the south-west wind is usually, though not always, the rain-bringer; north and east winds are generally fine-weather winds, and the west wind—often a strong one—tends to maintain whatever conditions were in force before it started to blow. A change of wind is the thing to watch for because it invariably means a change of weather, if only a clear windy day instead of a clear calm day. The wind backing, moving round from north to north-west for example, indicates a change for the worse. A veering wind—perhaps from south-west through west towards north-west—means better weather. The treacherous *Föhn* wind of the Alps, coming from south of south-west and preceded by massing clouds and strange colours in the sky, not only brings heavy snow or even rain high up but also has an insidious 'rotting' effect on the under-surface of snow-slopes.

Sky-signs in general need to be read with care. 'Red sky at night, shepherd's delight'—but if the red is accompanied by other gaudy colours it is not so good. A red sky at morning is a bad sign, but it must be differentiated from the pink dawn-suffusion which is not necessarily bad at all. The sun coming up over a clear horizon is good, over a belt of cloud bad. The clearness of the atmosphere during the day is a guide to coming weather, and though the unusual clarity of distant hills when your back is towards the sun is usually a good sign, it is bad to see them strikingly clear when you are facing the sun.

The importance of avoiding bad weather on a mountain is often not obvious to beginners in climbing, though any experienced mountaineer will be able to enlighten them. In the host of books containing factual accounts of mountaineering there are plenty of instances of the vital part played by mountain weather in the climber's sport; and no one who has read Gwen Moffat's book *Two-Star Red* will doubt the potential dangers of bad weather in British hills. The section on *Exposure* in Chapter Six of this book will have hinted at the penalties of allowing the weather to get the upper hand on a mountain, and in Chapter Ten some of the changes it can make in the surfaces with which the climber deals are described. It will be plain from the foregoing paragraphs, however, that weather forecasting is at best a calculation of probabilities, and that everyone who goes on mountains is likely to experience bad weather at some time or another, in great or small degree. To say that one should then retreat at once to the valley is a counsel of perfection; as often as not there will be many hours of exposure to the bad weather before the retreat is safely achieved. The climber's defence against this is special and adequate clothing. This part of his equipment is at least as important as the equipment he uses for actual climbing on rock or snow.

One of the chief problems in devising the perfect outfit of clothes for a mountaineer is the range of temperature he is likely to encounter. Even in Britain he will sweat heartily all the way up the sheltered flank of his mountain, only to encounter freezing wind on the crest; and in the Alps he may start in the icy cold of dawn, wilt in tropic heat on the glacier, and then suffer in a below-zero storm on the summit. The factor of weight prevents him from carrying the several outfits that would be ideal for all the variations of the conditions he meets with. Up to twenty or thirty years ago the compromise of an unlined tweed suit— jacket, waistcoat, and breeches—was the best available; it recognised the need for the body to 'breathe' when hot sun or exertion heated it, and to be kept warm by the retention of warm air in the woven fabric when temperatures were much lower. That *wind* was the great enemy on mountains was realised then, but no defence had been found against it. The invention of close-weave fabrics that are almost completely impervious to wind ousted the tweeds and brought us nearer the ideal, and the design of these windproofs, improved when it was realised that survival in bad storm conditions depended on the reduction of heat-loss, was soon modelled on the Eskimo's hooded anorak. A modern mountaineer would no more begin his ascent without his windproofs than a dinghy sailor would race without his life-jacket.

The anorak is most efficient when it has no front zip or pockets. However, the 'kangaroo' pocket across the chest is so useful that it can be included, provided that there is a flap, arranged so that it cannot be blown open by a headwind, covering the zip-fastener of the pocket. The hood should be sewn on to the anorak and fit snugly round the face when the drawstring is pulled tight; but it should be roomy enough to go on over a woollen balaclava helmet. Climbers differ as to whether a drawstring at the waist, or one at the bottom edge of the anorak, is the better, and some have both. Ideally the anorak should be long enough to come well down over the buttocks, but it will not stay there during active climbing unless you have a strap and buckle between the legs holding it down. A thin fabric such as bri-nylon is very efficient for any form of mountaineering except rock-climbing where it can be torn easily in contact with rocks; proofed canvas or windproof cloth makes the rock-climber's anorak. Bri-nylon is not only nearly waterproof but very light, and this

makes it feasible to wear an ordinary tough anorak for normal climbing and to carry a complete
outer suit of bri-nylon (anorak and trousers together weigh just sixteen ounces) in the rucksack,
thus being very efficiently prepared for the worst
of mountain weather.

Getting wet through is the common lot of the
climber, in Britain at any rate. To wear completely
waterproof garments is no solution, because the
condensation of bodily heat on their inner surfaces can make the wearer as wet as the rain would
make him. But in fact the mere wetness is nothing
to worry about; it is the bodily chill resulting from
it that in bad conditions hastens the onset of
exhaustion and collapse from exposure. Heat-loss
is the danger, and as always wind is the prime
enemy, drawing the warmth out of the soaked
clothing as soon as the body tries to warm it. The
windproof anorak keeps the warmth in and the
wind out. There are circumstances (a long
enforced halt in foul weather, for instance) where
the disadvantages of a waterproof are outweighed
by its imperviousness, and some climbers are now
carrying a plastic cagoule, or long hooded smock,
as protection additional to the normal anorak.

Two lightweight anoraks are a better shield
against wind, cold, or rain than one heavy one,
and the same principle applies to the clothing

worn underneath. One heavy wool sweater is not so efficient as two good light shetlands, and these have the added advantage that one can be discarded for the better adjustment of body temperature. Underwear of the cellular sort is best, but the string vest—wholly admirable for conditions of dry cold—becomes as miserably uncomfortable as a wet dishcloth next the skin when you are wet through.

For the climber's lower half breeches are normally the wear, except for winter Alpine climbing or similar near-Arctic conditions where the constriction of the knee-lacing and stocking are best avoided in favour of ankle-length undertrousers with windproof outers. Whipcord for hardwearing breeches, wool for warmth, is the criterion. Corduroy or velvet cord is hopeless when wet. In all clothing restriction of blood circulation should be avoided as far as possible, the ideal defence against cold being a windproof outer envelope well sealed at neck and ankle, with loose cellular undergarments; thus braces are better than a belt, and there is great advantage in being able to loosen the waistband without the breeches collapsing round the knees. Avoidance of constriction round the feet is important in high Alpine climbing. Two pairs of thick wool socks make sufficient cushioning to allow the lacing to be tight enough round the ankle, and a pair of *stop-touts* or gaiters covering trouser-bottoms and boot-tops help to exclude snow which would melt and make the socks wet; but the boot itself must be roomy, especially round and above the toes. There should be space in front of all the toes, and you should be able to 'scrunch-up' the toes inside the boot without discomfort. Frostbite is the enemy you defeat by this means.

All woollen and cellular garments are less efficient protection when they are dirty, because dirt and grease clog the cells that retain the warm air. More obviously, a hole-y sweater is not so warm as it would be if it was conscientiously darned. These may seem small points, but the history of mountaineering is crowded with instances where maintenance of body-warmth was vital to survival. To a man battling with a snowstorm on a mountain warmth is at least as important as skill and experience in mountaincraft; and a warmth in such circumstances is synonymous with energy—the power (as it is defined in mechanics) to effect work.

Another small but important point is the stopping of the gap at the neck of the anorak. This gap is normally the body's chief breathing-place when the climber is producing excess heat by his exertions, and most people find a roll-neck sweater irksome and chafing. A wool scarf or a piece of towelling should fill the gap when cold or storm attacks. The finest scarf for the purpose is one made of mohair. Incidentally, the most vulnerable point of any anorak is the junction of the hood at the back, where both rain and cold wind seem somehow to make their first entrance. If a woollen balaclava is not worn, a loosely woven wool scarf round the neck and back of the head wards off the cold.

In Alpine mountaineering an inner wool mitt— thumb separate only —with an outer gauntlet of proofed canvas is recommended as the best covering for the hand. Unproofed leather, lined or unlined, freezes to steel hardness if it gets wet. On rock of any difficulty gloves, even fingerless mitts, inevitably reduce the prehensile efficiency of the hands; they should be put on only during halts and for belaying.

Finally, some notes on the safety-helmet, fast becoming standard climbing equipment for the Alps and now appearing very frequently on British crags. It is often the 'irresponsible neutral' that sends down falling stones in the Alps. Overnight frost freezes the moisture in a crack, expands as ice, pushes the rock fragments outwards but holds it ice-welded in place; the coming of the sun warms the rock-face and melts the ice, and the released rock or stone hurtles down. In Britain the irresponsibles are human, the increasing numbers of ignorant or careless scramblers who send rocks down accidentally or (sometimes) on purpose. The safety-helmet protects against that most dangerous of mountain injuries, a head wound or fractured skull, whether from a falling stone or from a fall on the climb. Such a helmet is usually made of tough resilient nylon, weighs less than eleven ounces, and costs £1 or a little more. When buying one, see that the harness attaching it to the head is designed to withstand a severe impact from an angle as well as from directly above.

# 10

# Rock and Snow Surfaces

If there is any distinction between the climber and the mountaineer, it may be this: that while the mountaineer appreciates and enjoys every sort of surface his mountain provides, the climber only begins to enjoy himself when he steps on steep rock or snow. With snow we include ice, since the ice of mountains is simply frozen and compacted snow.

Mountains present a great variety of surface, all of which are almost infinitely varied by changing weather or season. Hard snow and sound rock are merely the most exhilarating of them. The others are usually dismissed as easy ground, walker's terrain where the ability to set one foot in front of the other is the only skill required; but the inference that these less exciting surfaces are safe for the inexperienced is, in some cases, a false one. Steep grass, for instance, in Britain as well as in the Alps, has taken its toll of lives. There are plenty of long grass slopes as steep as many a rock buttress and with crags or boulder-scree at the bottom, slippery as glass in drought and nearly unclimbable when the turf has been moistened and hard-frozen in winter. Scree—a very variable surface—and the moraine of glaciers can be as fatal to a careless climber as a vertical precipice. But since in general the climber avoids grass and scree by a circuitous route which may be a path or the track to an Alpine hut (or, nowadays, a cable railway) he regards his climbing as beginning and ending with rock and snow.

Rock can occasionally be pronounced thoroughly sound or thoroughly unsound, but between these extremes there is a wide intermediate range. Rock that is sound in mass may weather into small flakes that break off under fingers and toes, unsound rock may have its detached fragments so arranged that it can be safely climbed when only downward pressure is used on them. A geologist or a very experienced mountaineer can assess the character of rock at sight; but for most of us a little knowledge and common sense, allied to the habitual testing of every hold before weight is rested on it, is sufficient safeguard. The scree below a rock-face can give warning of unsoundness above by the pallid fragments of recent falls, or the face itself may display the discolourations and obvious unstable strata that reveal its weakness. The white quartz intrusions in igneous rock, hard and firm though they appear to sight and touch, are always to be regarded with suspicion, for the junction between two different types of rock is the place where rain and frost and heat do their slow but progressive work of loosening. Vegetation on a cliff is not always a sign of bad rock. The heather and bilberry on such faces as Lliwedd and Tryfan in North Wales indicate merely the large ledges on a favourable 'lie' of the strata, though it should be noticed that heather growing on a vertical face with no ledges to speak of will be doing its own slow loosening by pushing its thickening roots behind a flake. A smattering of botany can assist by identifying flowering plants like Moss Campion and Mountain Avens, which grow on faces composed of unsound carboniferous rock.

On most British mountains the climber deals with igneous rock, a wide-embracing term that includes both sound and unsound surfaces. This rock is not difficult to judge for soundness. Its safe and solid buttresses have weathered into sharp-cut definite holds, and its softer portions have long ago disintegrated into gullies and scree. The rarer sandstone of the Torridon and other hills is nearly always very sound in mass, though its rounded surfaces have a thin patina of loose

T.A.B.O.C.—F

stuff that needs extra care. Millstone grit, the gritstone of British midland and northern outcrops,
is outstandingly sound; here the lack of clear-cut
holds and the rough grain of the rounded surfaces
demands a specialised technique based on fine balance above a pure friction hold, and the difficulty
is not greatly increased when the rock is wet. On
limestone, by contrast, rain makes all friction
holds quite untenable, especially on the harder
limestones like 'dolomite' limestone. The 'mountain limestone' of some cliffs is too unsound for
free-climbing and here the Artificial climber comes
into his own. Granite, a splendidly firm rough
rock, is less common in Britain than in the Alps,
where it gives long and superb routes like those on
the Aiguilles of Chamonix. The astonishingly
rough gabbro of the Black Coolin of Skye is a
delight for any climber whose fingertips can stand
up to the abrasion of its sound spicules, and here
the instrusions of black basalt make a complete
contrast. As with quartz, their appearance should
be regarded as the signal for extra caution, for
though these lines of 'trap rock' are in the main
firm the large crystals are continually being un-
dermined by weather. Also, the surface of basalt
is extremely smooth. To step from gabbro on to
wet basalt, as you do on the Cioch Gully route, is

like stepping from the surrounding wood floor of an ice-rink on to the skating surface.

Weather changes can affect the character of a rock surface enormously. The commonest effect, a shower of rain, puts up the standard of some routes into a higher grade, particularly with moulded-rubber soles. The onset of high wind makes delicate routes far more tricky and can be really dangerous when sudden gusts at gale force develop, as they may do on a partly sheltered face. Near the top of a long cliff, when the climbers are in direct shelter from a gale-force wind driving across the crest, reverse gusts striking upwards from behind them may catch a man off balance and dislodge him from his holds. In British winter and spring climbing as in the Alps the formation of *verglas,* a thin film of ice caused by moisture freezing rapidly on the rocks, may make even an easy rock climb hard and dangerous; in such circumstances climbers have removed their boots and climbed in woollen socks to escape from their quandary. A more insidious difficulty arises when new snow begins to fall on steep rock. Apart from its peculiarly numbing effect on groping fingers, it solidifies and then freezes under pressure, so that the powdered foothold safely used by the Leader has become a ledge of ice by the time the Second Man uses it. No further explanation is needed of why some climbers still prefer nails in wintry conditions, or why the Mountain Rescue Handbook states emphatically that 'Vibram soles are quite unsuitable for Scottish mountaineering at all times in winter and spring and in certain conditions in summer as well'. On an all-snow route, or an Alpine ascent of mixed rock and snow, Vibrams are always preferred although there may be places and conditions on the route where a nailed sole would be safer; nails have the bad quality of conducting cold to the foot, while soles of moulded rubber insulate against frostbite.

Snow surfaces are almost infinitely variable. The obvious variation, between very soft snow and very hard snow, is not the only range of difference. There is soft dry snow (powder snow) and soft wet snow; snow that has a hard crust and soft powder beneath and is safe but exhausting to climb on, and 'windslab' snow that is ready to start the most dangerous sort of avalanche. And other kinds and combinations of kinds, additional to the rapid changes that can take place in each according to the changing conditions of the day. Only long experience can bring a comprehensive knowledge of mountain snow; and it is here that the British-trained climber marvels at the Alpine guide who seems to know instinctively when easy-angled snow is dangerous or a steep-angled soft slope safe for climbing.

New-fallen snow must thaw and regelate in order to make a good climbing surface; before it has done this, it is liable to avalanche from any slope steeper than fifteen degrees. Thus a heavy snowfall on Alpine peaks puts them 'out of condition' for some time, possibly for several days, until regelation has made the snow firm and compact. The angle at which new snow will adhere depends on the undersurface. Whether it is wet snow or powder snow that has fallen during the climber's day, he never trusts it as footing. He discovers with his axe what sort of surface it is lying on, and if this is ice or old hard snow he must cut through the new surface and make all his steps in the old. When, as sometimes happens, he has to ascend or descend a slope of doubtful snow, he takes a vertical line, straight up or down; to climb on a wide slant, or to traverse across such a slope, greatly increases the danger of starting a snow slide. New snow lying on rock will have to be cleared step by step and the rock-holds beneath it used. On these unstable snow surfaces crampons are a positive danger; if they are not taken off, they must be cleared regularly and carefully of the snow that balls up between the points.

The action of the sun during the day changes all snow surfaces that are exposed to it, but in different degrees according to their angle and aspect. At dawn after a good-weather night in the Alps, all snow will probably be hard and firm, making fast walking and safe climbing possible. If the surfaces are already soft at dawn, it may be due to the *Föhn* whose unnaturally warm air breathes across the glaciers, and it will mean hazardous and very laborious snow-climbing if the ascent is continued. In normal good weather the horizontal surfaces (such as snow-covered glacier) and slopes at easy angles will soften much more than steeper snow-slopes because they receive the direct rays of the sun; on the descent at noon or afternoon these slopes will be toilsome and awkward, though not necessarily dangerous, while the snow-covered glacier will be both laborious and full of hidden dangers. The high snow plateaus marked *firn* or *ewig Schnee* on the Alpine maps are always to be avoided after the sun has reached them, for they will be exhausting morasses. By keeping round their edges, where the snow begins its upward slope and so only receives the sun-rays at an angle, firmer footing can be found. On an undulating snow plain a good leader can halve the time and labour for his party by planning his route to use the east or north sides of the undulations, where the snow will be less soft.

Wind affects snow-slopes in its own way. On

the side of a peak that has been sheltered from a strong wind the snow will be softer and more liable to avalanche than on the exposed flank, where the wind will have removed unstable patches and hardened the surface superficially. This crust, an exhausting nuisance when it forms on level surfaces because it lets the climber into soft stuff beneath, is often sound and safe enough for climbing at a steep angle. It must be distinguished from 'windslab', a condition of hard thick surface slabs formed above a soft and unstable undersurface and liable to avalanche. Windslab, however, is not a common formation in summer though to be guarded against in winter and spring.

Lastly, some notes on British snow surfaces. It was remarked in Chapter Four that good snow-climbing as found in the Alps has no real counterpart in British winter hills, where you must head for Ben Nevis at Easter to get the best short stretches of Alpine-type climbing. All the same, many British climbers naturally make the best use they can of snow when it falls and lies on the mountains of Cumberland or Wales. The conditions of thaw followed by regelation are not so common here as in the Alps and more often than not a snow ascent in Britain turns out to be a scramble on slush. But when the long steep slopes of really good snow do occur the safe and exhilar-

ating climbing (safe, that is, from the firmness of
the surface) is often accompanied by a danger
rarely met with on Alpine snow: the shallowness
of the layer. Failing any suitable protruding rocks,
the climber depends on his axe belay for safety.
At least two-thirds of the axe length should go into sound snow for an anchor belay, and quite
often there is not this depth of snow; the axe
spike hits loose scree a foot or so down and can
then give, at best, what has been called a 'psycho-
logical belay'—a belay giving no practical assurance of safety. Moreover, on steep open slopes
in Britain the snow is not infrequently thinner on
the upper and more exposed part of the slope. If
this added risk is taken, the climbers should be
sure of their competence and exercise special care.

Thin snow lying on steep hard-frozen scree is
as slippery as ice and less easy to climb or descend
safely. Grass declivities that have been lightly
snow-covered, cleared by thawing, and then re-
frozen, are particularly treacherous, though a fall
and slide on them generally results in nothing
more serious than bad bruising. Gullies where the
snow lies deep and has had time to get into condition provide the best British snow-climbing,
but it should always be remembered that the
snow may become hard ice before the climb is
over.

11

# Glaciers

In all high-mountain climbing glaciers play a
most important part. Occupying as they do the de-
pressions between the ridges of a peak, or even
forming part of the mountain-face that is to be
climbed, they are more often than not the climber's route to higher things. Most Alpine ascents
begin with a glacier, even if it is only used as part
of the way up to a hut; and every mountaineer
should know the basic theory of glaciers and their
behaviour in order to use them safely.

The glacier begins high up where the masses of
*névé,* the permanent snow which is being continually deposited, become so heavy as snow-ice
that they break away and thrust slowly downwards. The break occurs usually as a more or
less continuous line along the upper part of the
mountainslope. This is the *bergschrund* (*rimaye*
to the French climber) a very large crack or crevasse between the static *névé* and the downward-
moving ice. It follows that below the *bergschrund*

the ice, in motion over an uneven slope of rock, will buckle and crack as its bed humps up or tilts to one side or the other. The cracks thus formed are crevasses. Some glaciers lie in an almost level bed and are hardly crevassed at all, but most conform to the geography-lesson description of 'river of ice', flowing smoothly in flat straight stretches, becoming rough round bends, and falling over rocky steps in their beds. A level glacier at a widening of its course is likely to have its crevasses lengthways, their direction parallel to its flow. On a bend the crevasses on the outer side of the curve will be large and transverse—across the line of flow—while those on the inner side will be closed by the pressure and perhaps thrust up into steep crests of ice. Over a drop in the bed there will be transverse crevasses, big and irregular if the drop is steep. A long steep drop results in an ice-fall, where the crevasses themselves are broken and splintered into unstable ice-towers, *séracs*. The glacier may end in an ice-fall, but an Alpine glacier more commonly ends in a snout of ice well down towards the valley, with its river issuing from it.

The higher reaches of a glacier are often 'wet' glacier, a term which means covered with snow. The snow covers or bridges the crevasses, presenting a smooth and apparently firm surface. Here lies the chief danger to mountaineers, especially on a descent late in the day or in warm '*Föhn weather*'. Lower down the glacier the ice will probably be free from snow, with all its chasms revealed. This is 'dry glacier', a safer place for climbers, who can see and plan a good route through the maze of crevasses. This lower ice is often very far from dry. In hot weather a flat surface may be inches deep in melt-water and slush, and quite often a deep and swift-flowing stream presents the glacier-walker with a difficult and unexpected obstacle.

Rock debris falling from the mountain-flanks on either hand is deposited on the moving glacier and borne down with it, so that in the course of time two long and often regular mounds of stones are formed along its edges. These are the lateral moraines. Sometimes the best route on a glacier lies along the crest of a moraine, and here special caution is necessary. The moraine looks like an innocent heap of scree, where a false step would merely allow the foot to settle firmly on the stone beneath; but in fact there is black ice, water ice, under the moraine stones, which are very loosely attached and can occasion a bad or even fatal fall.

Where two glacier valleys meet, the junction of the two ice-streams is nearly always extremely difficult, if not impossible, to negotiate. The tur-

moil of jostling crevasses and pushed-up *sêracs*
has no practicable through-route. The same thing
results when both sides of a wide glacier's bed tilt
towards each other, forcing two systems of crevasses together and causing impenetrable chaos in
which cubical islands of ice with impassable crevasses on every side are typical obstacles. A wide
detour or a traverse along the rock wall above are
likely to be the speediest ways of passing such
places.

The routes to Alpine huts often involve walking on glacier. To reach the Réquin or the Cou-
vercle huts above Chamonix, for instance, the ice
of the Mer de Glace is used for part of the way—
'dry' glacier where the crevasses are so large and
plain that parties do not usually rope up. On these
passages the track is generally obvious and little
or no route-finding is required. It is a very different matter to work your way up or down a snow-
covered glacier on the mountain. Once you are
out on the ice it is next to impossible to see the lie
of the crevasses or plan your route ahead. An un-
conscionable time can be spent—particularly in
descent—casting back and forth with interminable
crevasses opening at your feet on every line.
Knowing something of the probabilities mentioned
in the foregoing paragraphs, you can do a little
better by estimating, from the formation of the

glacier, where the most hopeful line will be. If the glacier makes a bend to the right, you will expect wide crevasses on the left and an awkward jumble of ice on the right, and head for a possible through-route between the two. If the glacier humps into convex form you will travel cautiously, suspecting longitudinal crevasses under the snow running in the direction you are walking. A zigzag progress is probable here, for crevasses have to be crossed at right-angles and the danger of having the whole party at once walking above a masked crevasse is obvious. When the glacier drops in an icefall route-finding on the ascent is easier, for the tilted surface displays its ledges and cracks as you approach and you can head for the likeliest starting-point for getting up it. But on a descent the same place will be troublesome, because its details are invisible from above. Prior knowledge of the varying obstacles on a glacier that is to be used on your climb can save precious hours, and though glaciers change from season to season and even week to week, and some of their crevasses may open or close during a single day, you can often get invaluable information from a previous party. Another and most helpful source of information is your own observation.

Reconnoitring the glacier, or at least the start of a glacier route, is sometimes possible on the evening before the ascent. Arrived (for example) at the Vignettes hut for a traverse of Mount Collon, a wise climber will take the first opportunity of scanning the glacier which is in full view below the hut. This glacier has to be crossed in order to reach the foot of Mont Collon's west ridge, and the party will be setting out in the near-darkness of 3 a.m. or thereabouts, so it will be an enormous advantage to have in mind a safe and speedy route round those crevasses. He will also take a walk down from the hut to the edge of the glacier and back; nothing is so delaying and dis-heartening to a party than to make a false start at the very beginning of a climb.

From the summit he may well be able to look down on the glacier by which the last part of the descent will be made. This is an opportunity which should never be missed, for a glacier re-veals its secrets most readily when viewed from above. When a party is climbing from a centre, making ascents of several peaks in the same dis-trict, the first summit can provide invaluable data about all the glaciers in view, which may have to be used in ascent or descent of other peaks.

More often than not, a wet-glacier ascent is made in early morning before the sun has touch-ed the surface. In good weather the snow will be firm and crisp and the bridges sound above the hidden crevasses. The climbers are of course roped together and well prepared (see Chapter Five) and the Leader is continuously on the lookout for crevasses as they advance in single file. A snow-masked crevasse generally betrays its presence by a slight depression above its length, appearing as a long faint shadow on the white surface. Tinted snow-glasses make it easier to perceive this shadow. The Leader, using his axe shaft to probe the depth and firmness of the snow, may find that he can tread safely across the frozen snow-bridge. If he is at all doubtful, his Second takes an axe belay while he crosses. If the axe-probe discovers the snow to be too dubious or the crevasse too wide for crossing at that point, the party will have to move sideways, along the crevasse, until it narrows or the snow becomes firmer.

Open crevasses on wet glacier should be approached with caution, remembering that the typical crevasse is bottleshaped, wider under the surface than it is above, and that the snow verges may be undercut. A jump across may be possible, solving a problem and saving time, and in this case the Second takes a firm axe belay and is careful to allow the Leader plenty of slack rope when he makes his leap.

When an ice-fall has to be climbed, the art lies in selecting a route that is nowhere threatened by the possible fall of a *sérac* or ice-pinnacle. The debris of recent falls can often be discerned and this area avoided. In the early morning ice-falls are less likely to discharge falling blocks than after the sun has touched them, but *séracs* should not be trusted even when bound by sunless frost. On the other hand, a good eye for the architectural weaknesses of an ice-fall can take a party safely through it in doubtful conditions.

The *bergschrund*, marking the glacier's upper end and the beginning of *névé* slopes free from crevasses, is often bridged only in one or two places, which vary with season and weather. Here again the architectural eye can better judge the safety or otherwise of the bridge, an arch presenting a safer route than a flat snow-bridge. Careful belaying is always necessary when crossing a *bergschrund*. When there is no bridge, and a search along the big crevasse in both directions has found no easier crossing, it is sometimes possible to cut steps down the ice on one side until a step-across to the opposite wall can be made and a ladder of steps carved up that. Commonly the glacier is steep at this terminal point, and the upper lip of the *bergschrund* much higher than the lower, so that the bridge—if there is one—is at a steep angle. When the same bridge has to be used on the descent, later in the day, it must be remembered that the sun's heat is likely to have softened and weakened it. It is sometimes safer, then, to cross it by a downward slide, a glissade lying on the face or on the back; but the most careful judgement and belaying are needed if this is to be done.

The descent of the glacier after the climb is shown, by accident statistics, to be one of the Alpine climber's most dangerous passages—not so much because of the actual dangers as from the carelessness that seems to overtake even experienced mountaineers when the day's climbing is almost over. Long hours on the rope—as many as twelve hours sometimes—leads the party to take a chance and unrope on easy snow-covered glacier, trusting perhaps to their tracks of the morning, or those of some other party, to steer them safely past the hidden perils. But the sun will have weakened all the surface, and the solid footing that was stamped out in the firm snow of morning may very well have thinned to a few inches of melting snow over a crevasse. The rope is more than ever essential to safety, and the Leader's vigilance doubly necessary. This is so obvious that one might think any words of cautionary advice unnecessary; yet a weary party released from the tension of a steep descent will often unrope on the glacier, each man taking his own line on the soft but apparently harmless snow. I have been with a party of two ropes, each led by a senior Alpine Club member, when it was decided to unrope for the final trudge across wet glacier. I broke through into a hidden crevasse, though I was following the tracks of the others, and was only saved by the jamming of my very large rucksack between the ice-walls. Probably the intense afternoon heat which often hangs on a glacier, making so tremendous a contrast with the brisk keen air of the heights, has something to do with this strange relaxation of care on ground so plainly dangerous. But there is in fact no excuse for it.

# 12

# Mountain Leadership

The past quarter of a century has seen two major
changes in the attitude of the general public towards the use of British hills and mountains. The
first great change came just after World War II,
when rock-climbing ceased to be the culpable folly
of a few and became the approved and popular
sport of a multitude; the second and more recent
change was brought about by the realisation that
our home mountains offer an invaluable training-
ground for young people and even children. One
of the inevitable results of social security has been
the tendency to lose the individual self-reliance
and initiative which, in a competitive society, are
developed much more fully. As soon as social and
educational authorities perceived this danger they
looked for a remedy and found it in a tremendous expansion of open-air pursuits for the young,
especially by introducing them to mountaineering
in its milder forms of hill-walking, scrambling,
and easy rock-climbing. Today almost every

Local Education Authority that has not already established a mountain centre is seeking one. In addition, schools, big industrial firms, and youth clubs are following the same line, setting up bases in or on the verge of mountainous country whence parties of boys and girls set forth every week for their introduction to mountains. Before this mass invasion of the hills by youth, and now continuing parallel with it, individual teachers, scoutmasters and others were taking their own parties of youngsters on mountain treks. The new influx has revealed a grave danger—the shortage of competent leaders for such parties.

Many accidents and rescues (some of them in circumstances of almost criminal folly) brought very strong protests from experienced mountaineers, notably from the R.A.F. Mountain Rescue teams who had to deal with the results of bad leadership and adult ignorance. They suggested that the time had come for the institution of some form of test or check before a youth leader was permitted to lead his charges into the potential dangers of the hills. It was, and is, impossible to fence off the mountains from the reckless and incompetent; but already authorities of any standing have recognised the importance of the Mountain Leadership Certificate as confirming the competence of leaders and the safety of their young followers. The Certificate is issued by the Mountain Leadership Training Board, composed of representatives of the Central Council of Physical Recreation and the British Mountaineering Council, with some individual members, numbering among them Sir John Hunt. It will not be out of place to quote its requirements:

'To qualify for the Award a candidate must complete:

(*a*) an Introductory Course lasting at least one week at a training centre approved by the Training Board.

(*b*) at least one year's practical experience to follow (*a*) as a leader, assistant leader or group member of expeditions during weekends and holidays, details of which are to be recorded in a personal log book which will be available to candidates at a training centre, price 5*s*.

(*c*) a final week's Residential Training Course at an approved training centre during which an assessment of the candidate's ability will be made for the Certificate Award. Minimum Age Limits for Men or Women candidates: for entry to an introductory course, 18; for the Certificate Award, 20. A current certificate in First Aid of the St. John Ambulance Brigade or the British Red Cross Society is required before a Certificate can be awarded.

A series of four weekend courses or their
equivalent may be approved by the Board as an
Introductory Course.'
These requirements demonstrate very forcibly the
importance attached to competent mountain
leadership by those who know the mountains best.

It was one of the older foundations of climbing
that the mountain pastime was for adults only. Today a new 'foundation' has, clearly, to be added:
that no adult shall take children or youngsters on
mountains unless he or she is not only a competent leader of children but also a competent mountaineer. For this reason the final chapter of this
book—by no means the least important—
addresses the leader of youth as distinct from the
leader of a climbing party.

A large number of senior mountaineers, when
they are beginning to feel 'past it', gain a renewed
pleasure in their pastime by introducing a boy or
girl to rock-climbing. This is one of the less
hazardous forms of youth leadership. The climber
usually knows his youngster well, sees that he has
had some previous experience of walking and
scrambling on hills, makes sure he is properly
equipped. He chooses a first climb likely to be
within the child's powers and therefore well within his own. There is, however, one possibility of
serious danger which he rarely realises: if the un-

likely accident happens to him on the climb (as it can do even to the 'tiger' in his prime) his party will be in a far graver situation than if he were climbing with an adult. A boy of twelve cannot possibly arrest the fall of a twelve-stone leader, nor can he take any helpful action after the fall has occurred. The position of an injured climber in such circumstances would be as full of tragic possibilities as that of the child alone and guideless on the rock-face. Theoretically, the only safe way of giving a youngster a taste of rock-climbing is for him to be in charge of two adults, on the same rope with him; it is a theory too seldom put into practice.

With teenage boys or girls the problem is a little different, depending more on the individual youngster and his or her previous training. For instance, a leader might confidently undertake (as I have done) to introduce a pair of Senior Scouts to climbing, provided that they were both physically fit and had done some hill-walking. But a period of training and observation should be required before the rock-climbing venture, a minimum of two good days. On the first day, a longish mountain walk involving some rock scrambling without the rope; on the second, instruction in climbing and belaying on easy rocks; on the third

—but only if the pair have shown adequate competence on the practice rocks—a genuine climb on one of the classic Moderately Difficults. Senior Scouts are perhaps a special case, for they can usually be trusted to learn knots and rope systems quickly and use them accurately.

It is a mistake, often made, to take a young beginner up a Severe or Very Severe for his first rock climb. He may get the thrill of being on a hard and exposed face, but he will not *climb* it. He will miss the feeling of confidence in himself growing and still to grow, the final inner assurance that 'I could climb something a bit harder than that—and climb it safely, too', which is the soil from which all the great mountaineers have sprung.

But the problems of a youngster's first rock climb are simpler and more evident than those confronting the leader of a party of youngsters on a hill-crossing or mountain ascent. The dangers here are more subtle, and for that reason greater.

Not long ago I was descending alone along the narrow Crib Goch ridge of Snowdon. The so-called 'knife-edge' is a place whence no one of ordinary agility, possessing normally prehensile fingers, should fall; but a slip and fall on the north side would be certainly fatal, and on the south side could result in serious injury. It was a day of thick mist driving over the crest before a strong wind, visibility a dozen yards or so. On the narrowest part of the ridge I met a party of schoolboys, all between the ages of ten and twelve, all clad in ordinary leather shoes and blue raincoats. There were twenty-two of them, with two grown men—properly shod and dressed in anoraks—in charge. The wind was lashing the skirts of the raincoats up into the boys' faces, their inadequate shoes were sliding on the smooth mist-wet footholds. One of the leaders was in front, the other at the rear of the line; and the half-dozen boys in the middle were quite out of sight of either man. I watched the boys' faces from my perch below as they clutched and slid along above me. Some were enjoying it, others were scared and shaky; but all were very far from safe. Had one of those boys in the middle lost his nerve or his hand-hold, he could have tumbled to his death without either of the leaders even seeing him go. This is one example of the many instances of dangerous incompetence which all frequenters of British mountains see. The lesson, one of the first the youth leader must learn, is that the number in the party should always bear a reasonable proportion to the number of leaders. What the 'reasonable proportion' is will depend on the age and responsibility of the youngsters, their equipment, and the nature of the ground; but on places where a false or careless step could mean serious accident one adult to one child is not too many.

Equipment for mountains generally was dealt with in Chapter One, and what was there said about protection against mountain weather applies with greater force to children. Youngsters have not the same resistance to bad weather as adults have, either morally or physically. The Outdoor Pursuit centres mentioned earlier rarely send children out ill-equipped nowadays, but other young parties are too often badly shod and poorly protected. One of the most dangerous persons on our hills (he is still to be met with) is the schoolmaster who years ago—perhaps in his own school holidays—vastly enjoyed one or two ascents of a favourite mountain, always in fine weather. He naturally wants his class to have the same grand experience, and organises a trip by coach or train to climb the peak. '*We* climbed it in shorts and sand-shoes' is his characteristic phrase, and he pooh-poohs any suggestion that special equipment is needed. Wind and rain on the great day are not allowed to spoil his plans. Off up the mountain go the unprepared youngsters and their confident guide, to vanish in the mist—often without map or compass, for this type of leader usually sums up his route-finding in the words 'Just keep going till you reach the top'. The seeds of a thousand narrow escapes and several tragedies have been sown in this way. Their cause has nearly always been assigned to some quite unpredictable weakness on the part of one of the children or an accident resulting from a child's carelessness or disobedience; but in nine cases out of ten the sole responsibility for the mishap rests on the Leader.

Sound equipment goes a long way towards cancelling-out the effects of bad weather and poor route-finding. The lack of it, when a drenching rainstorm catches the youthful party on a high exposed place, can lead very quickly to exhaustion, careless walking, 'fed-up-ness', and consequent disposition to lag or otherwise ignore the Leader's commands—the likelihood of mishap being thereby increased tenfold. Unsuitable footwear not only increases the probability of a slip on steep places but also leads to weariness and pain in feet and legs, liability to twisted ankles, and unnecessary fright on wet slopes. A major difficulty here is that proper boots are expensive and children's feet still growing; a new pair every year or less is beyond the means of many parents. Rubber ankle-length shoes ('baseball' or 'basket-ball' type) are often used, and can be passed as just good enough in favourable conditions—in dry weather on an easy route or ascent by a track. In wet weather they invite trouble; in spring or autumn they should not be used. In winter children should not be taken on mountains at all.

The majority of large youth parties are nowadays adequately clothed and properly shod for their mountain ventures. But their leaders often appear unaware of the special precautions demanded for their charges. The basic principles laid down in Chapter One must be scrupulously adhered to and the leader should see that all the members of his party have at least read those principles or heard them read. The route to be followed should be chosen with regard to the strength, experience, and age of the party and a time-distance schedule (see Chapter Seven) made out for that route; if for some reason the party gets far behind schedule the Leader must *always* retreat while there is plenty of daylight for the return journey. An early start—earlier than you think really necessary—is invaluable with youngsters.

Before starting out from base a check of each child's equipment including spares and reserve food is an obvious necessity. Less obvious and more difficult is the duty of making certain that every youngster is physically ready for the climb; boys in particular will do their best to conceal any temporary lack of fitness—stomach upset or blistered heel, for example—because of their eagerness not to be left behind. Illness or lameness revealed high up on the mountain will at best mean a ruined day and at worst put the whole party in hazard. A leader must harden his heart in a discovered case of unfitness or inadequate equipment, and if there is no immediate remedy that member of the party must remain behind.

Two adult leaders should be the rule for a youth party of more than two or three even if the day's route is an easy one. This more than doubles the assurance of success and safety. If the senior leader already has the respect and affection of his followers he can always command their obedience, but in any case he must make it plain from the outset that he expects to be obeyed. For his own part he must consider the pace of the slowest member of the party and adjust his speed and resting-points accordingly. No straggling should be tolerated, and in mist the party should close up in single file with the assistant leader or a reliable teenager bringing up the rear. The numbers of any large party should be checked repeatedly, especially in mist or bad weather. It is incredibly easy, particularly with small children, for one of them to get lost. A striking illustration of this fact was a very recent all-night search, involving 250 searchers and an R.A.F. helicopter, for a small boy who had strayed from a party of twenty-six crossing rough but not high mountain terrain on a clear sunlit afternoon. The boy was out all night and was discovered next morning safe at a farmhouse. The party had arrived at a wire fence over which the children had to be lifted. The small boy was the first over, and the leaders, their attention concentrated on lifting the others over, failed to notice that he had gone on by himself and taken the wrong route. He was out of sight in less than two minutes among the rocks and heather, and the rest of the party did not miss him until they got back to base. At such halts—indeed, at every halt—a count of heads should be a leader's invariable rule.

These severities may seem a little hard as an introduction to a pastime that can provide more pure joy and freedom from care than any other. But the first and most fundamental lesson to be learned about mountains is that they are not child's play. The early climbers called the Alps 'the playground of Europe', but they meant a playground for exceptionally tough and experienced men. It is the task of a youth leader on mountains to see that his charges learn the respect due to the high places in all their varying moods, while at the same time taking care not to destroy their growing delight in a new and priceless freedom. It is not an easy task. But it is very well worth doing.

# Index

A cloth-bound edition of this book, entitled *The Foundations of Climbing*, is available from the original publishers, Messrs Stanley Paul Ltd, at 21s.